OLD MO

HOROSCOPE AND ASTRAL DIARY

•

TAURUS

foulsham
London   New York   Toronto   Sydney

foulsham

The Publishing House, Bennetts Close,
Cippenham, Berks SL1 5AP

ISBN 0-572-02352-9

Printed in Great Britain at
Cox & Wyman Ltd, Reading

CONTENTS

1   Old Moore's Horoscope   5
     & Astral Diary - Introduction

2   Here's Looking at You   6
     A Zodiac Portrait of Taurus
     (21st April - 21st May)
     The Intention - Your Virtues -
     Your Vices - Living a Happy Life

3   What's Rising ?   10
     Your Rising Sign and Personality

4   Taurus in Love & Friendship   18

5   The Moon And The   19
     Part it Plays in Your Life

6   Retrograde Mercury   23

7   Moon Signs   24
     More About The Moon   30

8   The Moon Through The Zodiac Signs   32

9   The Astral Diary   36

10   At a Glance   186
     Your Rising Sign

11   The Zodiac at a Glance   188

12   The Zodiac, Planets   189
     And Correspondences

OLD MOORE'S HOROSCOPE AND ASTRAL DIARY

Old Moore's Horoscope and Astral Diary represents a major departure from the usual format of publications dedicated to popular Sun-sign astrology. In this book, more attention than ever before has been focused on the discovery of the 'real you', through a wealth of astrological information, presented in an easy to follow and interesting form, and designed to provide a comprehensive insight into your fundamental nature.

The interplay of the Sun and Moon form complex cycles that are brought to bear on each of us in different ways. In the pages that follow I will explain how a knowledge of these patterns in your life can make relationships with others easier and general success more possible. Realising when your mind and body are at their most active or inactive, and at what times your greatest efforts are liable to see you winning through, can be of tremendous importance. In addition, your interaction with other zodiac types is explored, together with a comprehensive explanation of your Sun-sign nature.

In the Astral Diary you will discover a day-to-day reading covering a fifteen-month period. The readings are compiled from solar, lunar and planetary relationships as they bear upon your own zodiac sign. In addition, easy-to-follow graphic charts offer you at a glance an understanding of the way that your personal life-cycles are running; what days are best for maximum effort and when your system is likely to be regenerating.

Because some people want to look deeper into the fascinating world of personal astrology, there is a section of the book allowing a more in-depth appraisal of the all-important zodiac sign that was 'Rising' at the time of your birth. You can also look at your own personal 'Moon Sign' using simple to follow instructions to locate the position of this very significant heavenly body on the day that you were born.

From a simple-to-follow diary section, on to an intimate understanding of the ever-changing child of the solar system that you are, my Horoscope and Astral Diary will allow you to unlock potential that you never even suspected you had.

With the help and guidance of the following pages, Old Moore wishes you a happy and prosperous future.

HERE'S LOOKING AT YOU

A ZODIAC PORTRAIT OF TAURUS
(21st APRIL - 21st MAY)

The typical misrepresentation of Taurus is that of a thick-set Bull-like character, with bulbous protruding eyes and a short neck. In fact, nothing could be further from the truth since, ruled as they are by Venus, Taureans tend to be amongst the best looking people in the zodiac. Even amongst the most ordinary of these individuals there is something inherently attractive. The tendency is towards dark hair and eyes, though the complexion is light and clear and the skin is particularly fine. The whole impression is one of fullness, with a squarish face, full mouth and lips, a strong purposeful jaw and well sculpted features.

Taurus possesses the best speaking voice of any sign, since the throat and the vocal chords are under the rulership of the Bull. Although not especially witty or entertaining speakers, Taureans are simply pleasant to listen to, with a harmonious quality that lifts any oration. Taurus produces good singers, actors and professional speakers of all types. Of course, there are two sides to every coin and this region of the body is the one that is inclined to give problems if life style is ignored.

Venus is the natural ruler of the sign of Taurus, a certain indicator of the natural sense of harmony, beauty and refinement the Bull accepts as being second nature. The Taurean home is inclined to be light and airy, full of pastel shades and reflecting the great outdoors, which is the natural home of all these bovine counterparts.

In terms of general health, the Taurean is inclined to be fairly robust, a little too much so if some care is not exercised when it comes to diet. It is a sad fact of all people ruled by Venus that an early, natural beauty of form can be turned into a parody of poise and elegance by a life of over-eating and a failure to keep generally fit and in trim. Chronic disorders are few here and the nervous system, though often misused, does tend to be fairly strong. This is aided by the Bull's refusal to be rushed or forced into anything.

THE INTENTION

The word tangible is defined as perceptible by touch, and what drives Taurus on is the need to experience the heights and depths of physical reality. This is achieved via the favourite channels of the sign; acquisition of money and possessions, a love of food and drink and general sensuality. It is fair to say that as an Earth sign, Taurus is rooted in the realms of the materialistic most of the time, its desire being to give form to the surrounding energies in the universe, to make things permanent and secure. This makes Taureans interested in tangible realities, rather than the creative energy that precedes them. Because of this it is not unusual to find the Bull participating in forms of art that result in a three-dimensional representation of subject matter, as is the case with sculpture. Taureans also make fine mechanical engineers, and, because of their natural country rulership, are often to be found working on farms or in market gardens. The Bull is attracted to nature in all its forms, another legacy of the Earth element, and also the love of beauty inherent in the planet Venus.

Through the five physical senses the Taurean experiences the world at large and is often artistic enough to translate what it takes in, especially through the medium of fine-art, design, interior decorating, even through the kind of muscular creativity exemplified by the Blacksmith.

Taureans are generally attracted to religion in its most basic form, if at all, and can happily experience their version of God through the colours of a painting, the key changes in a symphony, the taste of freshly cooked fish and chips, or a beautifully formed human body. All is grist to the mill as far as the Bull is concerned.

YOUR VIRTUES

The more colourful facets of the Taurean personality are expressed through a warmth and friendliness that is genuine and sincere; and you, the observer, realises that you are dealing with someone who values the integrity of your personality. If you are a phoney however, Taurus will spot you a mile away. It cannot abide superficiality in anyone, or those pretending to be something that they are not. Mother Nature is a governing factor in the Bull's approach to life. Synthetic anything tends to be shunned, and healthy, fresh food in opposition to frozen or processed are invariably the option. The home of the Taurean is inclined to reflect a knowing elegance and it is true to say that the average discerning Taurean would choose one really good item of furniture in preference to a house filled with plywood.

The orientation towards quality in people is also evident. When Taurus is happy and secure with the position it occupies in the world at large, it would be difficult to envisage meeting a more gentle or charming individual. There is a steady dependability and an air of refinement within this personality, so that it is not at all hard to lean on the solidity under-pinning this earthiest of signs. You won't be let down if you do, Taurus enjoys a chat as much as anyone, but it is steadfast and loyal, willing to suffer torture sooner than to betray a confidence.

The Bull can be bold and fearless, and it may come as a surprise to realise that medals for bravery under fire are more likely to be won by a Taurean than by any other sign of the zodiac. The reason for this seems to lie in the Bull's loyalty to its friends and also in its temper. It takes great effort to annoy this character, though once you succeed - look out. Taurus fights willingly for its family or friends, knows no limits to strength or staying-power and can usually be relied on to come out on top. As far as success is concerned, dogged determination is the key to riches with this character.

YOUR VICES

Victorian astrologers invariably portrayed Taureans as having a bad memory, a basically hostile attitude (albeit masked by a quiet, unassuming manner) and very little imagination in the sphere of creative pursuits. All of this reflects the inherent bestiality of the bovine sign that the historical astrologers believed they could recognised. Fortunately this is far from the truth, which is not to suggest that the average Taurean belongs in the realms of the saints - far from it. Animal cunning might not be far from the mark, but the Bull has a very good memory, especially if owed money or in the throes of bearing a grudge. Taurus can wait to get even, and often does, though the Bull will only take so much baiting before it reacts instinctively and with great force. Either way, upset a Taurean just once and it could take you a long time to get back into their good books again.

A lack of imagination certainly does not appear to be the case when it comes to an appreciation of beauty in all its forms, though can become evident in the Taurean tendency to stick doggedly to what it understands and appreciates, be it a certain district to live in, or a particular television programme to watch. Taureans can be possessive, especially in relationships, over-careful with money, generally acquisitive and also brooding if upset or crossed.

LIVING A HAPPY LIFE

Seen from your own point of perspective, there is nothing especially complex about your nature. You take life pretty much in your stride and would be practical enough to get by, even if you found yourself living on the proverbial desert island. It is the world of realities that takes your fancy, with all its attendant sights, smells, flavours and other sensual experiences.

Taurus rules the throat and to some extent the chest. These are the areas that will give you the most problems if you try to do too much or push that cast iron constitution beyond sensible limits. Your diet should be wholesome and pure and you need plenty of rest, especially if you are called upon to exercise your mental faculties to any great extent.

There is little doubt that, when crossed, you can be one of the most stubborn individuals in the zodiac. Up against another Taurean you could find yourself struggling for years without ever reaching a satisfactory conclusion. Nevertheless, you are especially patient and will generally achieve your objectives by dint of perseverance and the drive to work long and hard.

Your relationships are usually secure and happy. You need a partner who is not so flighty that their movements become a blur to you, though one who is stimulating enough to offer some of the lightness of touch that your own nature can lack, especially if you find yourself living under pressure. Family is quite important and the Bull takes well to looking after children. You could be rather authoritarian in your approach to younger people and should try hard to remain young; it's far too easy for your sometimes heavy sign to get stuck in its ways and to indoctrinate your children with your own prejudices. Friends are not easily formed but will probably stick with you through thick and thin once they do come along.

WHAT'S RISING

YOUR RISING SIGN AND PERSONALITY

Perhaps you have come across this term 'Rising Sign' when looking at other books on astrology and may have been somewhat puzzled as to what it actually means. To those not accustomed to astrological jargon it could sound somewhat technical and mysterious, though in fact, in terms of your own personal birth chart, it couldn't be simpler. The Rising Sign is simply that part of the zodiac occupying the eastern horizon at the time of your birth. Because it is a little more difficult to discover than your sun-sign, many writers of popular astrology have tended to ignore it, which is a great shame, because, together with the Sun, your Rising Sign is the single most important factor in terms of setting your personality. So much so, that no appraisal of your astrological nature could be complete without it.

Your Rising Sign, also known as your 'Ascendant' or 'Ascending Sign' plays a great part in your looks - yes, astrology can even predict what you are going to be like physically. In fact, this is a very interesting point, because there appears to be a tie- in between astrology and genetics. Professional Astrologers for centuries have noted the close relationship that often exists between the astrological birth chart of parents and those of their offspring, so that, if you look like your Mother or Father, chances are that there is a close astrological tie-up. Rising signs especially appear to be handed down through families.

The first impression that you get, in an astrological sense, upon meeting a stranger, is not related to their sun-sign but to the zodiac sign that was rising at the moment they came into the world. The Rising Sign is particularly important because it modifies the way that you display your Sun-sign to the world at large. A good example of this might be that of Britain's best- known ex- Prime minister, Margaret Thatcher. This dynamic and powerful lady is a Libran by Sun-sign placing, indicating a light-hearted nature, pleasure loving and very flexible. However, Baroness Thatcher has Scorpio as her Rising Sign, bringing a steely determination and a tremendous capacity for work. It also bestows an iron will and the power to thrive under pressure.

WHAT'S RISING?

Here lies the true importance of the Rising Sign, for Mr Thatcher almost certainly knows a woman who most other people do not. The Rising Sign is a protective shell, and not until we know someone quite well do we start to discover the Sun-sign nature that hides within this often tough outer coat of astrological making. Your Rising Sign also represents your basic self-image, the social mask that is often so useful; and even if you don't think that you conform to the interpretation of your Ascendant, chances are that other people will think that you do.

The way that an individual looks, walks, sits and generally presents themselves to the world is all down to the Rising Sign. For example, a person possessed of Gemini Rising is apt to be very quick, energetic in all movements, deliberate in mannerisms and with a cheerful disposition. A bearer of a Taurean Ascendant on the other hand would probably not be so tall, more solid generally, quieter in aspect and calmer in movement. Once you come to understand the basics of astrology it is really very easy to pick out the Rising Signs of people that you come across, even though the Sun-sign is often more difficult to pin down. Keep an eye open for the dynamic and positive Aries Rising individual, or the retiring, shy but absolutely magnetic quality of of the Piscean Ascendant. Of course, in astrology, nothing is quite that simple. The position of a vast array of heavenly bodies at the time of birth also has to be taken into account, particularly that of the Moon and the inner planets Mercury and Venus. Nevertheless a knowledge of your Rising sign can be an invaluable aid in getting to know what really makes you tick as an individual.

To ascertain the exact degree of your Rising sign takes a little experience and recourse to some special material. However, I have evolved a series of tables that will enable you to discover at a glance what your Rising Sign is likely to be. All you need to know is the approximate time of your birth. At the back of the book you will find the necessary table related to your Sun-sign. Simply look down the left-hand column until you find your approximate time of birth, am or pm. Now scan across the top of the table to the place where your date of birth is shown. Look for the square where the two pieces of information connect and there is your Rising Sign. Now that you know what your Rising Sign is, read on, and learn even more about the fascinating interplay of astrological relationship.

TAURUS WITH TAURUS RISING

As with all people who share the same Rising sign and Sun sign, you would be considered by the world at large to be very typical of your part of the zodiac. Kind and understanding, you can on occasions also be very stubborn, especially if you are crossed over something that you see to be of particular importance. Once you have made your mind up to something, there is no force in the world strong enough to distract you or cause you to wander from your chosen path.

Taureans are usually creative and are lovers of beauty. This is doubly true in your case, so it is very important that you are able to create the sort of surroundings that you find to be comfortable and harmonious. You can toil long and hard to achieve your objectives and generally win through in the end. It is possible that you will occasionally be accused of lacking imagination, mainly because you know what you like and tend to stick to it. You make a good friend and a faithful partner.

TAURUS WITH GEMINI RISING

Here the slow, plodding, methodical Bull takes a back seat, in favour of the get-up-and-go quality of the Twins; at least that is how it is likely to appear to the world at large. Sensitive types may consider that there is something about you that just doesn't ring true, because they are picking up on the very real reserve that underpins that gregarious exterior. Only those that know you very well would be fully in tune with your occasional silences.

You like to think of yourself as being logically minded, rational and methodical, even though you often wander off into the netherworld of dreams and intuitions. The combination is rather a strange one, not least of all because the quieter Taurean is liable to be swamped by Gemini, making it difficult for the two qualities to be reconciled harmoniously. The Gemini side of your nature is always wanting to be at the forefront of things, and especially to be communicating, and yet you are enough of a Bull to keep your counsel over issues that you do not feel qualified to comment upon. It's all a little confusing, not least of all for you, making for a life that can be rather difficult on occasions. In your lighter moments however you can enjoy the best of both worlds.

TAURUS WITH CANCER RISING

You make a great fuss of your friends, perhaps because deep inside you have the feeling that they belong to you. Certainly you have enduring relationships that tend to last a lifetime, and you can be guaranteed to offer a warm welcome, congenial chat and a warm fire whenever pals turn up. Looking after others is the Cancerian way, amplified in this case by the presence of Taurus, which has an overriding need to maintain the status quo. Be careful that you don't stifle, when in reality you merely seek to nurture. Not everyone wants to have their life organised in the way that you find so instinctive.

You can be fairly reserved when faced with people who you don't know all that well, being quite shy and vulnerable to slights. However, outsiders seldom penetrate the tough exterior that represents both the hide of the Bull and the shell of the Crab, and it is from within the realms of your own intimates that hurts can be generated. The most important emphasis of all is on security. In a quiet and unassuming way your life is filled with successes.

TAURUS WITH LEO RISING

Far be it from me to accuse anyone of almost total self love, but let us face it, you do come quite close. That dignified Leonine exterior is certain to get you noticed. This is not a problem, in fact you actively seek the attention that so naturally comes your way. Nevertheless you are generous, warm-hearted and very brave. There is great power within your nature to do almost anything that you turn your mind to, you have courage, fortitude and endurance..

What you really need is a greater insight into the fact that not everyone in the world at large thinks about things in quite the same way that you do. Sometimes you show a distinct lack of patience with those individuals who dare to contradict your point of view and despite your generous and noble spirit, you can be a little obsessive about being in the right. You have a very strong desire nature, inclining you towards some jealousy and possessiveness, though you are loyal, protective and loving, particularly when you feel that it is your duty to take a particular individual under your wing. Getting some enjoyment from your life could be a problem sometimes.

TAURUS WITH VIRGO RISING

With this double Earth sign combination you typify your Sun sign of Taurus in most respects. Thus within you is evident all the conservative, level-headed qualities of the Bull. On top of this however there is great adaptability, which, it might be argued is the one thing that Taureans tend to lack. You are quite able to bend with the wind of change, and can achieve singly greater success in most areas of your life as a result. Communication is possible through the influence of Mercury-ruled Virgo, even though no Earth sign person could be considered to be from the most chatty area of the zodiac.

There is a tendency for you to see things in purely black and white terms, insisting that there is a rational explanation for almost everything. This is a belief that you can administer with a nit picking persistence, often to the annoyance of more flexible types. Everything in its place is certainly your motto and woe betide the people who have the courage to disagree. For all this you are loving, and free with advice and practical help.

TAURUS WITH LIBRA RISING

Libra sits comfortably with almost any sign, though few more harmoniously than that of Taurus. You graduated from the charm school of life at a very early age. With the most subtle of persuasion you manage to acquire all the things that the Taurean within you desires and other people seem grateful that they have had the chance to assist you on your way. You are a natural diplomat and peace-maker, filled with Venusian charm and able to turn most circumstances round to your own advantage.

The presence of Libra means that you are not as earthy as the typical Taurean would be, and this means that there is significantly more flexibility within your nature. Look for interests that involve you with others, work in a complaints department and you may even have people apologising to you that they have bought your shoddy goods. Your conversation can be shallow on occasions, but never dull, meaning that you are the life and soul of any party that you choose to attend. Watch out for a slightly greedy streak, especially where food is concerned.

TAURUS WITH SCORPIO RISING

This can be a rather heavy combination, with a fixed and often inflexible attitude that allows little in the way of compromise once you have made your mind up to any particular course of action. In short, you know what you like and what you want, so that it takes considerable effort on the part of others to find any degree of flexibility within you. On the reverse side, you are absolutely loyal, would stick to your friends through thick and thin and are unlikely to let the little idiosyncrasies of others prevent you from backing them up.

With Taurus and Scorpio together, there is a double dose of sensuality, and the emphasis for you is on the pleasures generated by, and owing to, the five senses. This means that you are fond of food and drink, home comforts and probably sex. You don't over-intellectualise any situation but are never-the-less a very deep thinker. Passions are reserved for those people who share your very private world, those who can look deep inside that complex, brooding nature.

TAURUS WITH SAGITTARIUS RISING

This represents an interesting combination since your broad-minded and optimistic Sagittarian persona masks a rather parochial, somewhat stick-in-the-mud individual. Your Rising sign runs quite contrary to the intentions and desires of Taurus, so there is bound to be a degree of disparity within your nature. On some occasions the bright, warm and diffuse qualities of the Archer will predominate, so that you are good to have around, though there is a much quieter side to your personality too and an inherent need for solitude on occasions.

Security is always going to be important to you in one way or another, together with the need for firm roots. At the same time you love to be entertaining and also to know what makes the whole world tick. At times you are inclined to over-spend, a situation that, as in so many other things, creates conflict between the opposing qualities of your nature. When out and about in the world you do like to look and feel good and on those occasions when you may have had one glass of wine more than is really good for you, it is possible to observe the Archer making a bid for freedom. You don't really like to upset others but find this to be inevitable on occasions.

TAURUS WITH CAPRICORN RISING

Locked up in the practical world as you are, other less materialistic souls might find you rather dull and uninspiring on occasions. This is a feeling inspired by the sometimes sober and conservative image that you present. You can be sensitive to this, and the fact itself can lead to a sort of self-conscious striving and too much of a desire to be interesting.

Life is generally a serious business for you, though you are happiest when in control and in the company of people that you have come to know and trust. You have good managerial ability and are usually successful in a career sense. On a more personal level, you need the company of someone who looks at life in a more light-hearted way and can be greatly influenced for the good if your own rather darker nature is subjected to a fun-filled atmosphere for any length of time. To this end you may choose to associate with either Geminis or Sagittarians, both signs that would take you right out of yourself and find, below the surface, the fun-loving individual you can really be.

TAURUS WITH AQUARIUS RISING

With your ability to analyse anything and everything, you would make a really good scientist, in fact many of you probably already are. High-flying theories and philosophies; religious tracts or mystical parables are all grist to the mill of your active and constantly ruminating mind. Things have to make sense to you, though it is a sense that conforms to your own particular rational world view.

Aquarius Rising is often accused of being rather eccentric, even weird on occasions, not that you are especially bothered what other people are inclined to call you. You are happiest in social settings, where you always have something original and interesting to say. Your life-style is fairly normal, which may surprise others a little, though the people closest to you are aware that you can even be a traditionalist when the mood takes you. You are both a thinker and a doer, so much so that your combination of signs is often attracted to the practical side of teaching, where your various skills could all find a sensible means of expression. You will certainly never be short of friends, even if one or two of them turn out to be every bit as unusual as you are.

TAURUS WITH PISCES RISING

Yours is a deeply passionate and caring nature. It is true that you often look at the world through rose-tinted spectacles, for you really do want everything in you life to be coated in glamour, beauty and pleasantness. Life doesn't always come up to your expectations for certain, but you make an excellent job of smoothing out the rough edges, not least of all with your optimism. Helping others is almost an integral part of your life and there are no lengths to which you would refuse to go in order to support someone for whom you really cared.

It is true that you can on occasions be something of a hedonist, happy to escape into a paradise of your senses (often including gluttony and sloth). Many people with this combination seek to find solace and comfort in stimulants of one sort or another, disguising their excesses from the world by overlaying them with a sense of respectability. Only learn to control such excesses and yours can be a contented life. A good, sound relationship could be vital.

TAURUS WITH ARIES RISING

In many respects you are a fairly typical Sun Taurus; how you differ lies mainly in your rather dynamic and spirited approach to life. There are occasions when your caution and reserve disappear altogether, as the placid Bull is transformed into the quick-tempered Ram. These sudden changes of character can come as a complete surprise to the people around you. You do possess Taurean thoroughness, which combined with the driving success coming from the direction of the Ram can make you a force to be reckoned with. In times of stress or difficulty you really come into your own and may well have been the type of person who could turn the course of a battle in former, more violent days.

Your approach to others could appear to be rather un-subtle and cavalier on occasions, though you mean no harm and can work tirelessly on behalf of the ones you love. Even if you are inclined to railroad your ideas, it does so often mean that at least something is getting done. In this respect you are a destroyer of red tape, which could make you one or two enemies on your way through life. The Aries side of your personality is inclined to opt for regular change.

TAURUS
IN LOVE AND FRIENDSHIP

WANT TO KNOW HOW WELL YOU GET ON WITH OTHER ZODIAC SIGNS?

THE TABLES BELOW DEAL WITH LOVE AND FRIENDSHIP

THE MORE HEARTS THERE ARE AGAINST ANY SIGN OF THE ZODIAC, THE BETTER THE CHANCE OF CUPID'S DART SCORING A DIRECT HIT.

THE SMILES OF FRIENDSHIP DISPLAY HOW WELL YOU WORK OR ASSOCIATE WITH ALL THE OTHER SIGNS OF THE ZODIAC.

Love					Sign	Friendship				
	♥	♥	♥	♥	**ARIES**	☺	☺	☺		
♥	♥	♥	♥	♥	**TAURUS**	☺	☺	☺	☺	
			♥	♥	**GEMINI**	☺	☺	☺		
			♥	♥	**CANCER**	☺	☺	☺		
		♥	♥	♥	**LEO**	☺	☺			
♥	♥	♥	♥	♥	**VIRGO**	☺	☺	☺	☺	☺
		♥	♥	♥	**LIBRA**	☺	☺			
			♥	♥	**SCORPIO**	☺	☺	☺		
		♥	♥	♥	**SAGITTARIUS**	☺	☺	☺	☺	
♥	♥	♥	♥	♥	**CAPRICORN**	☺	☺	☺	☺	☺
			♥	♥	**AQUARIUS**	☺	☺	☺		
		♥	♥	♥	**PISCES**	☺	☺			

THE MOON AND THE PART IT PLAYS IN YOUR LIFE

In astrology the Moon is probably the single most important heavenly body after the Sun. It's unique position, as partner to the Earth on its journey around the solar system means that the Moon appears to pass through the signs of the zodiac extremely quickly. The zodiac position of the Moon at the time of your birth plays a great part in personal character and is especially significant in the build-up of your emotional nature.

SUN MOON CYCLES

The first lunar cycle deals with the part the position of the Moon plays relative to your Sun sign. I have made the fluctuations of this pattern easy for you to understand by means of a simple cyclic graph. It appears on the first page of each 'Your Month At A Glance', under the title 'Highs and Lows'. The graph displays the lunar cycle and you will soon learn to understand how its movements have a bearing on your level of energy and your abilities.

YOUR OWN MOON SIGN

Discovering the position of the Moon at the time of your birth has always been notoriously difficult because tracking the complex zodiac positions of the Moon is not easy. This process has been reduced to three simple stages with Old Moore's unique Lunar Tables. A breakdown of the Moon's zodiac positions can be found from page 24 onwards, so that once you know what your Moon sign is, you can see what part this plays in the overall build-up of your personal character.

If you follow the instructions on the next page you will soon be able to work out exactly what zodiac sign the Moon occupied on the day that you were born and you can then go on to compare the reading for this position with those of your Sun sign and your Ascendant. It is partly the comparison between these three important positions that goes towards making you the unique individual you truly are.

HOW TO DISCOVER YOUR MOON SIGN

This is a three stage process. You may need a pen and a piece of paper but if you follow the instructions below the process should only take a minute or two.

STAGE 1 First of all you need to know the Moon Age at the time of your birth. If you look at Moon Table 1, on page 21, you will find all the years between 1905 and 1996 down the left side. Find the year of your birth and then trace across to the right to the month of your birth. Where the two intersect you will find a number. This is the date of the New Moon in the month that you were born. You now need to count forward the number of days between the New Moon and your own birthday. For example, if the New Moon in the month of your birth was shown as being the 6th and you were born on the 20th, your Moon Age Day would be 14. If the New Moon in the month of your birth came after your birthday, you need to count forward from the New Moon in the previous month. Whatever the result, jot this number down so that you do not forget it.

STAGE 2 Take a look at Moon Table 2 on page 22. Down the left hand column look for the date of your birth. Now trace across to the month of your birth. Where the two meet you will find a letter. Copy this letter down alongside your Moon Age Day.

STAGE 3 Moon Table 3 on page 22 will supply you with the zodiac sign the Moon occupied on the day of your birth. Look for your Moon Age Day down the left hand column and then for the letter you found in Stage 2. Where the two converge you will find a zodiac sign and this is the sign occupied by the Moon on the day that you were born.

YOUR ZODIAC MOON SIGN EXPLAINED

You will find a profile of all zodiac Moon Signs on pages 24 to 29, showing in yet another way how astrology helps to make you into the individual that you are. In each daily entry of the Astral Diary you can find the zodiac position of the Moon for every day of the year. This allows you to also discover your lunar birthdays. Since the Moon passes through all the signs of the zodiac in about a month, you can expect something like twelve lunar birthdays each year. At these times you are likely to be emotionally steady and able to make the sort of decisions that have real, lasting value.

THE MOON AND THE PART IT PLAYS IN YOUR LIFE

NEW MOON TABLE 1

YEAR	MAR	APR	MAY	YEAR	MAR	APR	MAY
1905	5	4	3	1950	18	17	17
1906	24	23	22	1951	7	6	6
1907	14	12	11	1952	25	24	23
1908	3	2	1/30	1953	15	13	13
1909	21	20	19	1954	5	3	2
1910	11	9	9	1955	24	22	21
1911	30	28	28	1956	12	11	10
1912	19	18	17	1957	1/31	29	29
1913	7	6	5	1958	20	19	18
1914	26	24	24	1959	9	8	7
1915	15	13	13	1960	27	26	26
1916	5	3	2	1961	16	15	14
1917	23	22	20	1962	6	5	4
1918	12	11	10	1963	25	23	23
1919	2/31	30	29	1964	14	12	11
1920	20	18	18	1965	2	1	1/30
1921	9	8	7	1966	21	20	19
1922	28	27	26	1967	10	9	8
1923	17	16	15	1968	29	28	27
1924	5	4	3	1969	18	16	15
1925	24	23	22	1970	7	6	6
1926	14	12	11	1971	26	25	24
1927	3	2	1/30	1972	15	13	13
1928	21	20	19	1973	5	3	2
1929	11	9	9	1974	24	22	21
1930	30	28	28	1975	12	11	11
1931	19	18	17	1976	30	29	29
1932	7	6	5	1977	19	18	18
1933	26	24	24	1978	9	7	7
1934	15	13	13	1979	27	26	26
1935	5	3	2	1980	16	15	14
1936	23	21	20	1981	6	4	4
1937	12	12	10	1982	24	23	21
1938	2/31	30	29	1983	14	13	12
1939	20	19	19	1984	2	1	1/30
1940	9	7	7	1985	21	20	19
1941	27	26	26	1986	10	9	8
1942	16	15	15	1987	29	28	27
1943	6	4	4	1988	18	16	15
1944	24	22	22	1989	7	6	5
1945	14	12	11	1990	26	25	24
1946	3	2	1/30	1991	15	13	13
1947	21	20	19	1992	4	3	2
1948	11	9	9	1993	24	22	21
1949	29	28	27	1994	12	11	10

MOON TABLE 2		
DAY	APR	MAY
1	J	M
2	J	M
3	J	M
4	J	M
5	J	M
6	J	M
7	J	M
8	J	M
9	J	M
10	J	M
11	K	M
12	K	N
13	K	N
14	K	N
15	K	N
16	K	N
17	K	N
18	K	N
19	K	N
20	K	N
21	L	N
22	L	O
23	L	O
24	L	O
25	L	O
26	L	O
27	L	O
28	L	O
29	L	O
30	L	O
31	L	O

MOON TABLE 3						
M/D	J	K	L	M	N	O	P
0	AR	TA	TA	TA	GE	GE	GE
1	TA	TA	TA	GE	GE	GE	CA
2	TA	TA	GE	GE	GE	CA	CA
3	TA	GE	GE	GE	CA	CA	CA
4	GE	GE	GE	CA	CA	CA	LE
5	GE	CA	CA	CA	LE	LE	LE
6	CA	CA	CA	LE	LE	LE	VI
7	CA	CA	LE	LE	LE	VI	VI
8	CA	LE	LE	LE	VI	VI	VI
9	LE	LE	VI	VI	VI	LI	LI
10	LE	VI	VI	VI	LI	LI	LI
11	VI	VI	VI	LI	LI	SC	SC
12	VI	VI	LI	LI	LI	SC	SC
13	VI	LI	LI	LI	SC	SC	SC
14	LI	LI	LI	SC	SC	SA	SA
15	LI	SC	SC	SC	SA	SA	SA
16	LI	SC	SC	SA	SA	SA	CP
17	SC	SC	SA	SA	SA	CP	CP
18	SC	SA	SA	SA	CP	CP	CP
19	SA	SA	SA	CP	CP	CP	AQ
20	SA	CP	CP	CP	AQ	AQ	AQ
21	SA	CP	CP	AQ	AQ	AQ	PI
22	CP	CP	AQ	AQ	AQ	PI	PI
23	CP	AQ	AQ	AQ	PI	PI	PI
24	CP	AQ	AQ	PI	PI	PI	AR
25	AQ	PI	PI	PI	AR	AR	AR
26	AQ	PI	PI	AR	AR	AR	TA
27	PI	PI	AR	AR	AR	TA	TA
28	PI	AR	AR	AR	TA	TA	TA
29	PI	AR	AR	TA	TA	TA	GE

AR = ARIES TA = TAURUS GE = GEMINI
CA = CANCER LE = LEO VI = VIRGO LI = LIBRA
SC = SCORPIO SA = SAGITTARIUS CP = CAPRICORN
AQ = AQUARIUS PI = PISCES

RETROGRADE MERCURY

Before we see how the various zodiac positions of the Moon can have a bearing on you in a day to day sense, we need to look at another particularly important factor in your life, namely Retrograde Mercury.

A retrograde planet is one that appears, when viewed from the Earth, to be moving backwards through space. Of course this state of affairs is quite impossible, since planetary orbits around the Sun maintain only one direction. The reason that planets sometimes appear to be travelling backwards is due to the unique orbital position of the Earth within the solar system. When a planet seems to be running retrograde it is merely a line of sight effect caused by the relative positions of the planets at any given point in time. All of the planets, with the exception of the Moon, which is a satellite of the Earth and not strictly speaking a planet in its own right, can run retrograde. In the case of the larger planets, from Jupiter outwards, the retrograde periods can sometimes last many weeks.

Astrologers have always been fascinated by retrograde planetary movement and pay great attention to it, especially when constructing personal birth charts. However, in our lightening fast lives, no retrograde position is more important than that of tiny Mercury, which orbits closer to the Sun than any other planet in the solar system.

Mercury is the natural ruler of communication and one of the most obvious effects of its retrograde movement is that most forms of human interaction can suffer a little as a result. This can have a bearing on all human beings and it is amazing how often international negotiations, treaties and the like undergo setbacks if undertaken whilst Mercury is retrograde. In a more personal sense you will need to be aware on such days that it will be harder to get your message across to others. Greater tact and diplomacy are recommended and some patience in your general dealings with the world at large.

A further word of warning relates to mechanical objects, especially those such as computers, which also deal with communication. If you experience a difficulty in this direction, it will almost certainly occur whilst Mercury is retrograde. Such trends are seldom severe, but where you see the symbol ♦, immediately prior to the Moon Age Day on any Astral Diary entry, some slight precautions would be no bad thing.

MOON SIGNS

MOON IN ARIES

You have a strong imagination and a desire to do things in your own way. Showing no lack of courage you can forge your own path through life with great determination.

Originality is one of your most important attributes, you are seldom stuck for an idea though your mind is very changeable and more attention might be given over to one job at once. Few have the ability to order you around and you can be quite quick tempered. A calm and relaxed attitude is difficult for you to adopt but because you put tremendous pressure on your nervous system it is vitally important for you to forget about the cut and thrust of life from time to time. It would be fair to say that you rarely get the rest that you both need and deserve and because of this there is a chance that your health could break down from time to time.

Emotionally speaking you can be a bit of a mess if you don't talk to the folks that you are closest to and work out how you really feel about things. Once you discover that there are people willing to help you there is suddenly less necessity for trying to tackle everything yourself.

MOON IN TAURUS

The Moon in Taurus at the time you were born gives you a courteous and friendly manner that is likely to assure you of many friends.

The good things in life mean a great deal to you for Taurus is an Earth sign and delights in experiences that please the senses. This probably makes you a lover of good food and drink and might also mean that you have to spend time on the bathroom scales balancing the delight of a healthy appetite with that of looking good which is equally important to you.

Emotionally you are fairly stable and once you have opted for a set of standards you are inclined to stick to them because Taurus is a Fixed sign and doesn't respond particularly well to change. Intuition also plays an important part in your life.

MOON IN GEMINI

The Moon in the sign of Gemini gives a warm-hearted character, full of sympathy and usually ready to help those in difficulty. In some matters you are very reserved, whilst at other times you are articulate and chatty: this is part of the paradox of Gemini which always brings duplicity to the nature. The knowledge you possess of local and national affairs is very good, this strengthens and enlivens your intellect making you good company and endowing you with many friends. Most of the people with whom you mix have a high opinion of you and will stand ready to leap to your defence, not that this is generally necessary for although you are not martial by nature, you are more than capable of defending yourself verbally.

Travel plays an important part in your life and the naturally inquisitive quality of your mind allows you to benefit greatly from changes in scenery. The more you mix with people from different cultures and backgrounds the greater your interest in life becomes and intellectual stimulus is the meat and drink of the Gemini individual.

You can gain through reading and writing as well as the cultivation of artistic pursuits but you do need plenty of rest in order to avoid fatigue.

MOON IN CANCER

Moon in Cancer at the time of birth is a most fortunate position since the sign of Cancer is the Moon's natural home. This means that the qualities of compassion and understanding given by the Moon are especially enhanced in your nature and you cope quite well with emotional pressures that would bother others. You are friendly and sociably inclined. Domestic tasks don't really bother you and your greatest love is likely to be for home and family. Your surroundings are particularly important and you hate squalor and filth.

Your basic character, although at times changeable like the Moon itself, depends upon symmetry. Little wonder then that you are almost certain to have a love of music and poetry. Not surprising either that you do all within your power to make your surroundings comfortable and harmonious, not only for yourself, but on behalf of the folk who mean so much to you.

MOON IN LEO

You are especially ambitious and self-confident. The best qualities of both the Moon and the Sign of Leo come together here to ensure that you are warm-hearted and fair, characteristics that are almost certain to show through no matter what other planetary positions your chart contains.

You certainly don't lack the ability to organise, either yourself or those around you, and you invariably rise to a position of responsibility no matter what you decide to do with your life. Perhaps it is just as well because you don't enjoy being an 'also ran' and would much rather be an important part of a small organisation than a menial in a larger one.

In love you are likely to be lucky and happy provided that you put in that extra bit of effort and you can be relied upon to build comfortable home surroundings for yourself and also those for whom you feel a particular responsibility. It is likely that you will have a love of pleasure and sport and perhaps a fondness for music and literature. Life brings you many rewards, though most of them are as a direct result of the effort that you are able to put in on your own behalf. All the same you are inclined to be more lucky than average and will usually make the best of any given circumstance.

MOON IN VIRGO

This position of the Moon endows you with good mental abilities and a keen receptive memory. By nature you are probably quite reserved, nevertheless you have many friends, especially of the opposite sex, and you gain a great deal as a result of these associations. Marital relationships need to be discussed carefully and kept as harmonious as possible because personal attachments can be something of a problem to you if sufficient attention is not given to the way you handle them.

You are not ostentatious or pretentious, two characteristics that are sure to improve your popularity. Talented and persevering you possess artistic qualities and are a good home- maker. Earning your honours through genuine merit you can work long and hard towards your objectives but probably show very little pride in your genuine achievements. Many short journeys will be undertaken in your life.

MOON IN LIBRA

With the Moon in Libra you have a popular nature and don't find it particularly difficult to make friends. Most folk like you, probably more than you think, and all get together's would be more fun with you present. Libra, for all its good points, is not the most stable of Astrological signs and as a result your emotions can prove to be a little unstable too. Although the Moon in Libra is generally said to be good for love and marriage, the position of the Sun, and also the Rising Sign, in your own birth chart will have a greater than usual effect on your emotional and loving qualities.

You cannot live your life in isolation and must rely on other people, who are likely to play an important part in your decision making. Co-operation is crucial for you because Libra represents the 'balance' of life that can only be achieved through harmonious relationships. An offshoot of this fact is that you do not enjoy being disliked and, like all Librans are a natural diplomat.

Conformity is not always easy for you, because Libra is an Air sign and likes to go its own way.

MOON IN SCORPIO

Some people might call you a little pushy, in fact all you really want to do is live your life to the full, and to protect yourself and your family from the pressures of life that you recognise all too readily. You should avoid giving the impression of being sarcastic or too impulsive, at the same time using your energies wisely and in a constructive manner.

Nobody could doubt your courage which is great, and you invariably achieve what you set out to do, by force of personality as well as by the effort that you are able to put in. You are fond of mystery and are probably quite perceptive as to the outcome of situations and events.

Problems can arise in your relationships with members of the opposite sex, so before you commit yourself emotionally it is very important to examine your motives carefully and ensure that the little demon, jealousy, always a problem with Scorpio positions, does not cloud your judgement in love matches. You need to travel and can make gains as a result.

MOON IN SAGITTARIUS

The Moon in Sagittarius helps to make you a generous individual with humanitarian qualities and a kind heart. Restlessness may be an endemic part of your character for your mind is seldom still. Perhaps because of this you have an overwhelming need for change that could lead you to several major moves during your adult life. You are probably a reasonably sporting sort of person and not afraid to stand your ground on the occasions when you know that you are correct in your judgement. What you have to say goes right to the heart of the matter and your intuition is very good.

At work you are quick and efficient in whatever you choose to do, and because you are versatile you make an ideal employee. Ideally you need work that is intellectually demanding because you are no drudge and would not enjoy tedious routines. In relationships you anger quickly if faced with stupidity or deception, though you are just as quick to forgive and forget. Emotionally there are times when you allow your heart rule your head.

MOON IN CAPRICORN

Born with the Moon in Capricorn, you are popular and may come into the public eye in one way or another. Your administrative ability is good and you are a capable worker. The watery Moon is not entirely at home in the Earth sign of Capricorn and as a result difficulties can be experienced, especially in the early years of life. Some initial lack of creative ability and indecision has to be overcome before the true qualities of patience and perseverance inherent in Capricorn can show through.

If caution is exercised in financial affairs you can accumulate wealth with the passing of time but you will always have to be careful about forming any partnerships because you are open to deception more than most. Under such circumstances you would be well advised to gain professional advice before committing yourself. Many people with the Moon in Capricorn take a healthy interest in social or welfare work. The organisational skills that you have, together with a genuine sympathy for others, means that you are ideally suited to this kind of career or pastime.

MOON IN AQUARIUS

With the Moon in Aquarius you are an active and agreeable person with a friendly easy going sort of nature. Being sympathetic to the needs of other people you flourish best in an easy going atmosphere. You are broad minded, just, and open to suggestion, though as with all faces of Aquarius the Moon here brings an unconventional quality that not everyone would find easy to understand.

You have a liking for anything strange and curious as well a fascination for old articles and places. Journeys to such locations would suit you doubly because you love to travel and can gain a great deal from the trips that you make. Political, scientific and educational work might all be of interest to you and you would gain from a career in some new and exciting branch of science or technology.

Money-wise, you make gains through innovation as much as by concentration and it isn't unusual to find Lunar Aquarians tackling more than one job at the same time. In love you are honest and kind.

MOON IN PISCES

This position assures you of a kind sympathetic nature, somewhat retiring at times but always taking account of others and doing your best to help them. As with all planets in Pisces there is bound to be some misfortunes on the way through life. In particular, relationships of a personal nature can be problematic and often through no real fault of your own. Inevitably though, suffering brings a better understanding, both of yourself and of the world around you. With a fondness for travel you appreciate beauty and harmony wherever you encounter them and hate disorder and strife.

You are probably very fond of literature and could make a good writer or speaker yourself. The imagination that you possess can be readily translated into creativity and you might come across as an incurable romantic. Being naturally receptive your intuition is strong, in many cases verging on a mediumistic quality that sets you apart from the world. You might not be rich in hard cash terms and yet the gifts that you possess and display, when used properly, are worth more than gold.

MORE ABOUT THE MOON

In addition to your lunar birthdays, you can also gain a better understanding of the way cycles work in your life by keeping track of the Moon Age Day. You probably already know your Moon Age Day because it was the first stage of the process to establish your Moon's zodiac sign. If you have any doubts, look back to pages 19 and 20.

Keeping track of Moon Age Days can be very useful because you are likely to be at the peak of your personal life cycles at those times when the Moon reaches the same Moon Age Day each month as the one it had achieved at the time of your birth. So, for example, if you were born on Moon Age Day 12, you will find that around the same Moon Age Day each month your decision making skills are honed to perfection and that you find yourself in a position to take almost any bull by the horns. You can find the Moon Age Day to the right of the date on each daily entry in the Astral Diary.

THE MOON AGE QUICK REFERENCE TABLE

The situation goes much further however because all facets of astrology respond to 'resonances'. Certain Moon Age Days have much in common with your own, which makes those days more significant to you. Conversely, there are going to be Moon Age Days that are not so positive in relation to your own. To make the situation easier to understand you can look at the table on the page opposite. Scanning down the left hand column you can find your own Moon Age Day. How your own Moon Age Day relates to all the others can be seen by tracing along to the right.

+ Days harmonious with your own Moon Age Day and so find you more positive, anxious to make the most of every opportunity and keen to get ahead.

- Days are likely to be less favourable and represent days when it would not be sensible to take any unnecessary chances. You could feel just a little out of sorts and might be best avoiding too much exertion.

* Days occur only once each lunar month. Such times could well find you feeling on top form and very anxious to pitch yourself into any situation with absolute confidence. If you act with determination on * days, your chances of ultimate success could be that much higher.

MOON AGE QUICK REFERENCE TABLE

SIGNIFICANT MOON AGE DAYS

		+ Days	- Days	* Days
Y	0	4, 6, 12, 14, 19, 21, 25, 28	9, 16, 23	0
O	1	5, 7, 13, 15, 20, 22, 26, 29	10, 17, 24	1
U	2	0, 6, 8, 14, 16, 21, 23, 27	11, 18, 25	2
R	3	1, 7, 9, 15, 17, 22, 24, 28	12, 19, 26	3
	4	2, 8, 10, 16, 18, 23, 25, 29	13, 20, 27	4
O	5	0, 3, 4, 9, 11, 17, 19, 24, 26	14, 21, 28	5
W	6	1, 4, 5, 10, 12, 18, 20, 25, 27	5, 22, 29	6
N	7	2, 5, 11, 13, 19, 21, 26, 28	0, 16, 23	7
	8	3, 6, 12, 14, 20, 22, 27, 29	1, 17, 24	8
M	9	0, 4, 7, 13, 15, 21, 23, 28	2, 18, 25	9
O	10	1, 5, 8, 14, 16, 22, 24, 29	3, 19, 26	10
O	11	0, 2, 6, 9, 15, 17, 23, 25	4, 20, 27	11
N	12	1, 3, 7, 10, 16, 18, 24, 26	5, 21, 28	12
	13	2, 4, 8, 11, 17, 19, 25, 27	6, 22, 29	13
A	14	3, 5, 9, 12, 18, 20, 26, 28	0, 7, 23	14
G	15	4, 6, 10, 13, 19, 21, 27, 29	1, 8, 24	15
E	16	0, 5, 7, 11, 14, 20, 22, 28	2, 9, 25	16
	17	1, 6, 8, 12, 15, 21, 23, 29	3, 10, 26	17
D	18	0, 2, 7, 9, 13, 16, 22, 24	4, 11, 27	18
A	19	1, 3, 8, 10, 14, 17, 23, 25	5, 12, 28	19
Y	20	2,4, 9, 11, 15, 18, 24, 26	6, 13, 29	20
	21	3, 5, 10, 12, 16, 19, 25, 27	0, 7, 14	21
	22	4, 6, 11, 13, 17, 20, 26, 28	1, 8, 15	22
	23	5, 7, 12, 14, 18, 21, 27, 29	2, 9, 16	23
	24	0, 6, 8, 13, 15, 19, 22, 28	3, 10, 17	24
	25	1, 7, 9, 14, 16, 20, 23, 29	4, 11, 18	25
	26	0, 2, 8, 10, 15, 17, 21, 24,	5, 12, 19	26
	27	1, 3, 9, 11, 16, 18, 22, 25	6, 13, 20	27
	28	2, 4, 10, 12, 17, 19, 23, 26	7, 14, 21	28
	29	3, 5, 11, 13, 18, 20, 24, 27	8, 15, 22	29

THE MOON THROUGH THE ZODIAC SIGNS

The following pages should offer a little insight into the way that the Moon's various sign positions might have a bearing on your day to day life, whatever your own Moon sign.

MOON IN ARIES TODAY

When the Moon is in Aries you should be looking to commence new ventures. This is a good time to get things on the move and make up your mind about a change in attitude. There is a possibility that you will not be at your most patient during these periods, though the great advantage of the Moon is that it never stays in the same place for very long. It would be fair to suggest that the Moon in Aries brings a tendency to be easily discouraged, and especially so if you are born into a part of the zodiac that gives you a natural desire to achieve a great deal in a short period of time.

MOON IN TAURUS TODAY

A very much more cautious position of the Moon this, and there is absolutely no point in trying to rush anything whilst the Moon occupies the zodiac sign of Taurus. This is a lunar position that suits the sort of individual who is a careful and considered actor on the stage of life and so can prove to be quite stultifying to the more dynamic signs. Good for all forms of creativity, for example getting cracking with home decorations or simply for painting a picture. The Moon in Taurus is also fairly useful for finance, but only if you are willing to look at long-term investments.

MOON IN GEMINI TODAY

This turns out to be a very good time for getting almost any sort of message across and especially so when it comes to explaining how your emotional nature is running. It should not be difficult to speak words of love whilst the Moon is in Gemini and you might also be in a good position to talk others round to a point of view that you have been personally holding for quite a while. At work you should be firing on all cylinders and can afford to back your own hunches just as long as you are willing to explain to those around you the way that your mind is working.

MOON IN CANCER TODAY

Some would say that this is the best position of all for the Moon, since it is at its most comfortable when resting in the watery sign of Cancer. Chances are that you will find yourself at your most sensitive during this short period and you might have to be just a little careful about the way that you put your message across to others. All the same it is likely that you would be able to make those closest to you understand your deepest feelings, so that words of love often pass to and fro whilst the Moon occupies this sign. The only real word of caution is that you could give offence without realising that you have done so.

MOON IN LEO TODAY

If you are the sort of individual who loves to preen yourself in public and who is not afraid to tell it how it really is, then you will be a fan of the Moon in Leo. Confidence is not likely to be lacking and you are able to get much done, whilst at the same time maintaining a happy and comfortable frame of mind. Most people are likely to understand what you are trying to say and you can afford to put on something of a show during times such as this. The Moon in Leo could make you more brave than you usually consider yourself to be and you should take the bull by the horns in projects that are important to you.

MOON IN VIRGO TODAY

Definitely a time for the fussy members of life and the Moon in Virgo tends to make most people look more carefully at all manner of projects in order to make certain that the details are sorted out properly. There could be delays and whilst they last it might be useful to get things running smoothly at home, since you are able to put the domestic message across much more easily whilst the Moon occupies this sign. Confidence may not appear to be all that high and yet it is likely that you will get far more done at this stage than you might expect. Following up on projects from the past is good now.

MOON IN LIBRA TODAY

If you have been thinking about forming a new friendship, or even a deeper sort of attachment, you could not find a better time for doing so than during those short periods during which the Moon occupies the sign of Libra. This is a period during which you will be at your most diplomatic, so it is unlikely that you would offer any offence, no matter how important it seems to be to speak your mind. Your general attitude is likely to be flexible and you can easily turn your mind around to appreciate a point of view which might not normally be your own. Artistic endeavours are well highlighted and you may find that your dress sense is especially good.

MOON IN SCORPIO TODAY

This tends to be a very deep sort of period and one during which you may be standing still for a while, taking stock of life and being willing to allow yourself the time you need to get to know yourself a great deal better. You might take things to heart more than would usually be the case and that means that you have to be careful to listen carefully and not to react too quickly. Remember that the Moon in Scorpio tends to make you feel more intense and that to many people such periods are only short in duration. Give and take in a family sense comes easily to you during such interludes.

MOON IN SAGITTARIUS TODAY

A time to lift your mind above the mundane and to think about matters that would usually tax your mind a little. You are quite philosophical during these periods and should be able to get things sorted out easily, probably with the help of others, since most people respond quite positively when the Moon occupies the sign of the Archer. Reaching for the impossible might not be a bad thing since you might at least be able to get half way towards your objectives and should end up fairly satisfied with your efforts. Comfort and security are not all that important and there could be a definite urge for fresh fields and pastures new.

MOON IN CAPRICORN TODAY

There is no point in advising a steady attitude whilst the Moon is in Capricorn because that comes as standard. You certainly will not find yourself in a position to take too many chances and it is significant to observe how cautious stock markets tend to be during the Moon's stay in Capricorn. However, this is a very good time for planning and for settling any details that need great attention, so that, as a planning period, this position of the Moon could turn out to be one of the most useful of all. Quick reactions would probably be a waste of time though, if you take hours out to think about life.

MOON IN AQUARIUS TODAY

How quickly things can change and this is certainly the case as the capricious Moon moves from Capricorn into Aquarius. You should find yourself to be much more dynamic, willing to back your hunches to the hilt and able to see through the fog of life, straight into the heart of almost any situation. The innovators of the world tend to enjoy this position of the Moon the best of all, so that if you have a particularly positive idea, this proves to be the best period of all to do something about it. Keep any tedious projects on hold and go out for what you really want in life. The very next breeze to come along could blow you towards your chosen destination and since you don't want to miss it, spread your sail and get moving.

MOON IN PISCES TODAY

Really coming to terms with almost anything can be rather difficult during those times when the Moon occupies the sign of Pisces, so this might not turn out to be the most dynamic period of the them all. It isn't hard to see how other people might be thinking and it would be fair to suggest that many individuals are slightly more likely to be intuitive with Pisces helping the situation. To use this position the best, you need to look carefully at the psychological profile of your family and friends because this is the time when you are liable to see clear through to their motives. Reaction time is slow and you probably won't want to move any mountains, though to compensate you will find that those around you are as understanding in their attitude as you probably tend to be yourself.

THE ASTRAL DIARY

How the diagrams work

Through the *picture diagrams* in the Astral Diary I want to help you
to plot your year. With them you can see where the positive and
negative aspects will be found each month. To make the most of
them all you have to do is remember where and when!

Let me show you how they work . . .

THE MONTH AT A GLANCE

Just as there are twelve separate Zodiac Signs, so Astrologers
believe that each sign has twelve separate aspects to life. Each of
the twelve segments relates to a different personal aspect. I number
and list them all every month as a key so that their meanings are
always clear.

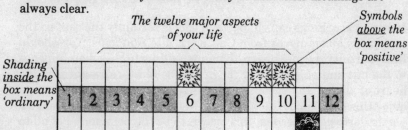

The twelve major aspects of your life

Symbols above the box means 'positive'

Shading inside the box means 'ordinary'

Symbol below the box means 'negative'

I have designed this chart to show you how and when these twelve
different aspects are being influenced throughout the year. When
the number rests comfortably in its shaded box, nothing out of the
ordinary is to be expected. However, when a box turns white, then
you should expect influences to become active in this area of your
life. Where the influence is positive I have raised a smiling sun
above its number. Where it is a negative, I hang a little rain cloud
beneath it.

YOUR ENERGY RHYTHM CHART

On the opposite page is a picture diagram in which I am linking
your zodiac group to the rhythm of the moon. In doing this I have
calculated when you will be gaining strength from its influence and
equally when you may be weakened by it.

If you think of yourself as being like the tides of the ocean then
you may understand how your own energies must rise and fall too.
And if you understand how it works and when it is working, then
you can better organise your activities to achieve more and get
things done more easily.

YOUR ENERGY-RHYTHM CHART

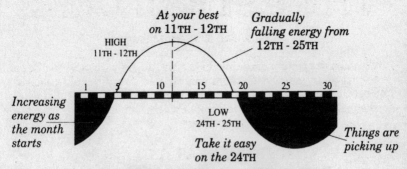

*At your best
on 11TH - 12TH*

*Gradually
falling energy from
12TH - 25TH*

HIGH
11TH - 12TH

1   5   10   15   20   25   30

*Increasing
energy as
the month
starts*

LOW
24TH - 25TH

*Take it easy
on the 24TH*

*Things are
picking up*

MOVING PICTURE SCREEN
Measured every week

LOVE, LUCK, MONEY & VITALITY

I hope that the diagram below offers more than a little fun. It is
very easy to use. The bars move across the scale to give you some
idea of the strength of opportunities open to you in each of the four
areas. If LOVE stands at plus 4, then get out and put yourself
about, because in terms of romance, things should be going your
way. When the bar moves backwards then the opportunities are
weakening and when it enters the negative scale, then romance
should not be at the top of your list.

*Love at +4
promises a
romantic
week*

*Not a good
week for
money*

← NEGATIVE TREND   POSITIVE TREND →

-5 -4 -3 -2 -1   +1 +2 +3 +4 +5

LOVE
MONEY
LUCK
VITALITY

*Below
average
for vitality*

*And your luck
in general
is good*

And Finally:

am ....

pm ....

The two lines that are left blank in each daily entry of the Astral
Diary are for your own personal use. You may find them ideal for
keeping a check on birthdays or appointments, though it could be an
idea to make notes from the astrological trends and diagrams a few
weeks in advance. Some of the lines carry a key, as above. These
days are important because they indicate the working of
'astrological cycles' in your life. The key readings show how best you
can act, react or simply work within them for greater success.

OCTOBER
1997

YOUR MONTH AT A GLANCE

The twelve numbered boxes represent the important areas in your life.
The key to the numbers you will find beneath the panel. A sun above the
number indicates that opportunities are around. A cloud below the
number, that you should be a bit defensive. Nothing above or below and
life will be pretty ordinary.

1	2	3	4	5	6	7	8	9	10	11	12

KEY

1 Strength of Personality
2 Personal Finance
3 Useful Information Gathering
4 Domestic Affairs
5 Pleasure & Romance
6 Effective Work & Health

7 One to One Relationships
8 Questioning, Thinking & Deciding
9 External Influences / Education
10 Career Aspirations
11 Teamwork Activities
12 Unconscious Impulses

OCTOBER HIGHS AND LOWS

Here, I show how the rhythm of the Moon will affect you this month. Like
the tide, your energies and abilities will rise and fall with its pattern.
When it is above the date line, go-for-it. When it is below the line you
should be resting.

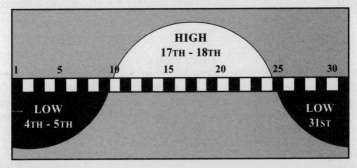

HIGH
17TH - 18TH

LOW
4TH - 5TH

LOW
31ST

6 MONDAY
Moon Age Day 5 • Moon Sign Sagittarius

am..

pm..

After a quiet sort of weekend you project yourself forward now with all the energy in the world. It's a good start to the week and can benefit you in a personal as well as a professional way. Many situations are tinged with potential excitement, almost from the very moment that you leap expectantly out of bed.

7 TUESDAY
Moon Age Day 6 • Moon Sign Sagittarius

am..

pm..

In some ways this turns out to be the physical and mental peak of the month. Now is certainly the time to take all those carefully laid plans and to put them into action. Taureans who feel that they have been put through the mill emotionally should now find the reactions of others to be far more positive generally.

8 WEDNESDAY
Moon Age Day 7 • Moon Sign Sagittarius

am..

pm..

There is a warm and intimate feel to life at present, and plenty going for you in the personal stakes. Look out for compliments that could easily be missed, but which are very important when you stop to think about them properly. Do try to avoid being carried away by what may be just infatuation however.

9 THURSDAY
Moon Age Day 8 • Moon Sign Capricorn

am..

pm..

Certain people seem to behave in what might seem to be a very unreasonable manner today. Of course it could be the way that you are feeling yourself, or a combination of circumstances. It would be better on the whole to watch the situation very carefully, but to decide not to react to it strongly.

10 FRIDAY
Moon Age Day 9 • Moon Sign Capricorn

am ....

pm ....
Taureans will not be put upon by anyone and this is certainly true now.
You are inclined to dig your heels in at the very thought of anyone
interfering and could be just a little too defensive for your own good.
Rules and regulations could also get on your nerves and you need to be
rather more patient.

11 SATURDAY
Moon Age Day 10 • Moon Sign Aquarius

am ....

pm ....
Although others declare that they have your best interests at heart, in
reality this may not be the case. You are deeply intuitive just at present
and that means that you look at all situations with a wise attitude, so
that the slightly less than typically Taurean reactions of yesterday will
not show.

12 SUNDAY
Moon Age Day 11 • Moon Sign Aquarius

am ....

pm ....
A decision regarding finances will be uppermost in your mind today and
this really is a good time for dealing with such matters. Projecting
yourself into hypothetical situations turns out to be something that you
are very good at now and there should be plenty of time to get your head
round past problems.

← NEGATIVE TREND							POSITIVE TREND →				
-5	-4	-3	-2	-1			+1	+2	+3	+4	+5
					LOVE						
					MONEY						
					LUCK						
					VITALITY						

13 MONDAY

Moon Age Day 12 • Moon Sign Pisces

am . . . .

pm . . . .

Expect a more favourable attitude generally and that is what you are likely to find. There are plenty of people around who are not only willing to listen to what you have to say, but who are also willing to take your opinions on board. Some Taureans will be taking the advantage of a stimulating new regime.

14 TUESDAY

Moon Age Day 13 • Moon Sign Pisces

am . . . .

pm . . . .

If things don't get done in quite the way you would wish, you can at least be certain that you will get round to them eventually. Start to plan ahead for the end of the year and make sure that your options are kept open socially for the end of this month. You may have to react quickly and decisively before long.

15 WEDNESDAY

Moon Age Day 14 • Moon Sign Aries

am . . . .

pm . . . .

A potentially interesting time is at hand, during which you should find that your emotional responses are strong but positive. It won't do any harm at all for others to know exactly how you are feeling and it might be more than sensible to speak your mind in personal situations. Watch and listen at work.

16 THURSDAY

Moon Age Day 15 • Moon Sign Aries

am . . . .

pm . . . .

Time spent alone is not at all wasted today. You have been in a more contemplative frame of mind for some time now and the phase comes to a head today. It's amazing how many house points you can score later, simply because you are willing to think things through now. You look especially attractive to new friends.

17 FRIDAY

Moon Age Day 16 • Moon Sign Taurus

am ....

pm ....
The arrival of the lunar high seems all the more powerful as you come
flying out of a period of personal withdrawal. Many demands are made
of you at the end of this working week and yet you are at ease with them
all. Not everyone displays the same enthusiasm for life that you do, but
you can take them on board too.

18 SATURDAY

Moon Age Day 17 • Moon Sign Taurus

am ....

pm ....
It's true that you tend to burn the candle at both ends today, and though
as a rule the advice would be to stop doing so, as long as the support of
the lunar high is around you can get away with it. The advice, once again,
is to look towards the end of the month and to get any social planning
sorted out now.

19 SUNDAY

Moon Age Day 18 • Moon Sign Gemini

am ....

pm ....
Be careful of unwise spending because there may not be quite as much
money about now as you would wish. You should soon find that money
matters ease, but for the moment be prepared to draw your horns in a
little. Sooner or later you are going to have to be straight with a friend
who is clearly not in the know!

← *NEGATIVE TREND*							*POSITIVE TREND* →			
-5	-4	-3	-2	-1		+1	+2	+3	+4	+5
					LOVE					
					MONEY					
					LUCK					
					VITALITY					

20 MONDAY
Moon Age Day 19 • Moon Sign Gemini

am...

pm...
People you come across are a source of significant news and great general interest today. In some ways it seems as if you have been asleep because there are things afoot that you know little or nothing about. Not only do you take the trouble to listen now but should be willing to have a good old chin wag yourself.

21 TUESDAY
Moon Age Day 20 • Moon Sign Cancer

am...

pm...
You should be able to get at least a couple of important tasks out of the way today and at the same time can afford to look carefully at your social life, which may need a shot of extra effort to get things moving. Confidence is not lacking and a reservoir of good will stands around you right now.

22 WEDNESDAY
Moon Age Day 21 • Moon Sign Cancer

am...

pm...
An association of Venus and Saturn in your chart now has a rather sobering effect on you, but that does not mean that it is negative. Although you may take life a little more seriously today, you are also being very responsible, which means others are that much more willing to follow your advice.

23 THURSDAY
Moon Age Day 22 • Moon Sign Cancer

am...

pm...
The best of life today comes from one-to-one relationships, which are clearly looking good for most children of Venus at present. Words of love and of wisdom come from the mouth of your partner, whilst single Taureans can expect romance to be playing a more positive role in their lives during the days ahead.

24 FRIDAY
Moon Age Day 23 • Moon Sign Leo

am . . . .

pm . . . .
A matter close to your heart can be discussed today, though you might not be all that happy about the people who are throwing the situation about. An injection of cash may seem well overdue but it is only a matter of time before things start to improve a little. An offer that you are looking for is already here.

25 SATURDAY
Moon Age Day 24 • Moon Sign Leo

am . . . .

pm . . . .
Look forward to a busy social life for the weekend and be prepared to leave more practical matters on the back burner for a while. You could end up being amazed at the progress you make, simply by being in the right place at the right time. There's little you can do about this, but life offers the opportunities.

26 SUNDAY
Moon Age Day 25 • Moon Sign Virgo

am . . . .

pm . . . .
With so much to remember and a host of new responsibilities likely to come your way at this time you push forward positively towards a horizon that you are not even really certain about. Get a few irritating chores out of the way if you can today because the week ahead is busy enough without them.

← *NEGATIVE TREND*								*POSITIVE TREND* →				
-5	-4	-3	-2	-1				+1	+2	+3	+4	+5
					LOVE							
					MONEY							
					LUCK							
					VITALITY							

27 MONDAY   *Moon Age Day 26 • Moon Sign Virgo*

am ....

pm ....
Your load appears to be considerably lighter at the start of this week,
probably because at least some of it has been passed onto its rightful
owners. You will not stand for people being unfair during this week,
especially if they are trying to pull the wool over your eyes. A very astute
Taurean greets this working week.

28 TUESDAY   *Moon Age Day 27 • Moon Sign Virgo*

am ....

pm ....
The repository of many of your hopes and wishes is evident between now
and the end of the month. All the prior planning and the free time you
left yourself socially come into play. With tremendous enthusiasm and
a great deal of energy you are able to make the most favourable
impression of all at this time.

29 WEDNESDAY   *Moon Age Day 28 • Moon Sign Libra*

am ....

pm ....
Everything you have worked so hard towards achieving is there for the
taking, though whether you choose to take advantage of the fact really
depends upon you. Some of your successes don't seem all that important
once you are able to enjoy them. All the same, you should find this to be
a particularly good day.

30 THURSDAY   *Moon Age Day 29 • Moon Sign Libra*

am ....

pm ....
Certain short-term plans need looking at again now and you may have
to modify your way of thinking if you do not want to be considered a stick-
in-the-mud. It's not that you are being particularly negative however
and perhaps it is best to proceed as you think fit, no matter what the
world has to say.

31 FRIDAY   *Moon Age Day 0 • Moon Sign Scorpio*

am..

pm..
Even the steepest mountain can be climbed if you just take the incline
one step at a time. It isn't how quickly you get things done that really
matters at the moment, but the way in which you are willing to about
your daily business. A smile is never far from your lips at present, which
in itself is important.

1 SATURDAY   *Moon Age Day 1 • Moon Sign Scorpio*

am..

pm..
The lunar low does slow things down a little, though almost certainly to
your advantage if you understand how pointless it is to swim against the
tide of life. You are fair and honest in your assessment of others and will
listen patiently to what they have to say. After that you will probably
ignore the advice!

2 SUNDAY   *Moon Age Day 2 • Moon Sign Scorpio*

am..

pm..
People do not always understand your off-beat sense of humour but if you
have to explain yourself the point of the joke is likely to be lost altogether.
You have the chance to get ahead in a purely personal manner at present
and will want to show certain people that you are quite capable at living
your own life.

← *NEGATIVE TREND*								*POSITIVE TREND* →				
-5	-4	-3	-2	-1			+1	+2	+3	+4	+5
					LOVE						
					MONEY						
					LUCK						
					VITALITY						

1997

YOUR MONTH AT A GLANCE

The twelve numbered boxes represent the important areas in your life. The key to the numbers you will find beneath the panel. A sun above the number indicates that opportunities are around. A cloud below the number, that you should be a bit defensive. Nothing above or below and life will be pretty ordinary.

1	2	3	4	5	6	7	8	9	10	11	12

KEY

1 Strength of Personality
2 Personal Finance
3 Useful Information Gathering
4 Domestic Affairs
5 Pleasure & Romance
6 Effective Work & Health

7 One to One Relationships
8 Questioning, Thinking & Deciding
9 External Influences / Education
10 Career Aspirations
11 Teamwork Activities
12 Unconscious Impulses

NOVEMBER HIGHS AND LOWS

Here, I show how the rhythm of the Moon will affect you this month. Like the tide, your energies and abilities will rise and fall with its pattern. When it is above the date line, go-for-it. When it is below the line you should be resting.

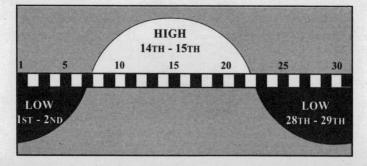

HIGH
14TH - 15TH

LOW
1ST - 2ND

LOW
28TH - 29TH

3 MONDAY
Moon Age Day 3 • Moon Sign Sagittarius

am ....

pm ....
It isn't really mixing with the world at large that benefits you at the moment but rather in a one-to-one sense with others. As a result of a very close co-operation with specific types you can make both professional and personal gains. A good time for small speculations and for planning ahead in a general sense.

4 TUESDAY
Moon Age Day 4 • Moon Sign Sagittarius

am ....

pm ....
Current trends mean that you might feel a little hampered by having to toe the line more than you would wish. This does not really hold you up in any long-term sense but you are bound to feel rather restricted when it comes to getting your own way. This is a pity since you know what you want very well.

5 WEDNESDAY
Moon Age Day 5 • Moon Sign Capricorn

am ....

pm ....
There may be an interesting twist or two in the offing today and you are likely to be playing the Sherlock Holmes in some way. It isn't that others deliberately try to mystify you, it's simply something that tends to happen. keep a generally open mind and try not to discriminate too much.

6 THURSDAY
Moon Age Day 6 • Moon Sign Capricorn

am ....

pm ....
Present aspects can put something of a damper on relationships, mainly because you are not looking at things quite as logically as you normally would. A tiring period could become obvious, but not if you are willing to make certain that work and rest go hand in hand, as they should for Taurus at the moment.

49

7 FRIDAY
Moon Age Day 7 • Moon Sign Aquarius

am ....

pm ....
One way or another it's all go today, not that you are likely to complain about the fact because you are getting so very much done. Friends and relatives alike seem more than willing to bear your point of view in mind and this could make you feel a little more important. Guard against too much controversy personally.

8 SATURDAY
Moon Age Day 8 • Moon Sign Aquarius

am ....

pm ....
The further you get into November, the more curious you seem to become about life in general. However, too much curiosity was not all that good for the cat and it might cause you a slight problem or two. There are times when it is simply best to accept things the way that they are and this is one of them.

9 SUNDAY
Moon Age Day 9 • Moon Sign Pisces

am ....

pm ....
Though you really do want to make your opinions heard over the general clamour of life, it isn't easy to do so right now. Shouting about things really does not help and you will just have to be as patient as you can. Others are probably more on your side than you think, even if it does not always seem that way.

← NEGATIVE TREND							POSITIVE TREND →			
-5	-4	-3	-2	-1			+1	+2	+3	+4	+5
					LOVE					
					MONEY					
					LUCK					
					VITALITY					

10 MONDAY
Moon Age Day 10 • Moon Sign Pisces

am . . . .

pm . . . .

If you find yourself at odds with anyone you can at least be certain that this is not a trend that will last for any length of time. Later in the day people seem to be much more helpful and to take your ideas at face value. Routines are easier to deal with and the start of the working week favours good luck.

11 TUESDAY
Moon Age Day 11 • Moon Sign Pisces

am . . . .

pm . . . .

A combination of quick thinking and intuition come to your aid today and make it less difficult for you to make the sort of progress that could have been lacking for the last few days. All in all you should be as bright as a button right now and easily able to make the best of impressions on the world at large.

12 WEDNESDAY
Moon Age Day 12 • Moon Sign Aries

am . . . .

pm . . . .

Don't expect too much of yourself today. The truth of the matter is that you have your own fish to fry in a personal sense and that others are more than willing to take some practical responsibilities on board. A good time for assessing specific matters and for laying down some specific plans.

13 THURSDAY
Moon Age Day 13 • Moon Sign Aries

am . . . .

pm . . . .

Before the end of the today the lunar high begins to show itself. If you are fairly positive in your attitude you can make the very best of present trends and should find little to hold you back in a general sense. Not everyone is as optimistic as you are, but it is only a matter of time before you bring them round.

14 FRIDAY

Moon Age Day 14 • Moon Sign Taurus

am ....

pm ....
It's clear that you have energy to spare now and that you will be doing all you can to get the decks cleared ahead of the weekend. Many situations can benefit from your personal touch and you will not have to try all that hard to succeed in a number of ways. Some specific overtures romantically are worth a second look.

15 SATURDAY

Moon Age Day 15 • Moon Sign Taurus

am ....

pm ....
Be careful that the things you say do not trigger off the sort of arguments that you did not intend. It would not be useful to cause rows or to take part in them today and you can do a great deal to be a peacemaker. There is plenty to keep you occupied at all levels, but especially so in a personal sense.

16 SUNDAY

Moon Age Day 16 • Moon Sign Gemini

am ....

pm ....
Things could seem a little unsettled in financial matters but this is a temporary situation and should not hold you back beyond today. You need to look at things realistically and not to allow your imagination to get the better of you. You show a great regard for someone who is new to your life.

← *NEGATIVE TREND*						*POSITIVE TREND* →				
-5	-4	-3	-2	-1		+1	+2	+3	+4	+5
					LOVE					
					MONEY					
					LUCK					
					VITALITY					

17 MONDAY   *Moon Age Day 17 • Moon Sign Gemini*

am ....

pm ....
Relationships seem a little more unsettled, as indeed do other aspects of your life just at the moment. Once again you are probably looking at things too closely for your own good and a more general over view would probably be better. Your creative skills have rarely been better, especially regarding home.

18 TUESDAY   *Moon Age Day 18 • Moon Sign Cancer*

am ....

pm ....
Look out the sort of people who have a similar view of life to the one that you hold yourself. This would be an ideal time for making new friends and for coming to terms more with the ones you already have. The level of general luck that attends your life is likely to be on the increase and romance also looks likely.

19 WEDNESDAY   *Moon Age Day 19 • Moon Sign Cancer*

am ....

pm ....
Most Taureans are quite impressionable at the moment and you are casting your eyes in the direction of people you really do admire. Now willing to take a few more chances you may even be making personal decisions that friends do not agree with. All the same you are inclined to do what you want at present.

20 THURSDAY   *Moon Age Day 20 • Moon Sign Leo*

am ....

pm ....
Outside circumstances prevent you from feeling as generally happy as you would wish. In fact there is really nothing of any consequence standing in your way and it is only your own frame of mind that gets in the way. As long as you remain quite open and flexible, present trends are not likely to get you down.

21 FRIDAY

Moon Age Day 21 • Moon Sign Leo

am ....

pm ....

Although you have been a little unsettled recently the situation now settles down and you begin to realise exactly why you have been feeling as you have. There is a purpose in all things and Taureans usually realise the fact. Getting on with others is now as easy as falling off a log, so you don't have to try too hard.

22 SATURDAY

Moon Age Day 22 • Moon Sign Leo

am ....

pm ....

A completely new phase gets underway in your life, thanks to the position of the Sun which enters your solar eighth house today. Things generally can be turned on their head, though you should be fairly certain that it is all for the best in the end. You really do need to take a hand in the process.

23 SUNDAY

Moon Age Day 23 • Moon Sign Virgo

am ....

pm ....

Perhaps you should take the opportunity to get a little more excitement into your life right now, even if it seems that you are taking a chance or two on the way. What is life without a little lack of caution now and again? Socially you are good to know and get on extremely well with different sorts of people.

← *NEGATIVE TREND*							*POSITIVE TREND* →				
-5	-4	-3	-2	-1			+1	+2	+3	+4	+5
					LOVE						
					MONEY						
					LUCK						
					VITALITY						

24 MONDAY
Moon Age Day 24 • Moon Sign Virgo

am ....

pm ....
You are very open to new social influences during this most extraordinary time and can gain a great deal from the many new contacts that come into your life. There are many different sorts of people who have a bearing on your life at present and you should relish the new interests that come with them.

25 TUESDAY
Moon Age Day 25 • Moon Sign Libra

am ....

pm ....
For the first time in several days the advice now is to keep to tried and tested paths. This might not please you too much now that you are really in gear but there are likely to be many tasks that need taking care of. In addition you have been stretching yourself more than is really good for you and may need a rest.

26 WEDNESDAY
Moon Age Day 26 • Moon Sign Libra

am ....

pm ....
A little restlessness overtakes you now and can only be dealt with out there in the big, wide world. There ought to be plenty to keep you occupied, not least of all personal relationships, which probably offer more now than at any stage this month. Not a period for gambling or for taking chances of any other sort.

27 THURSDAY
Moon Age Day 27 • Moon Sign Libra

am ....

pm ....
The lunar low brings a quieter and more contemplative phase and you may already be laying down plans for the weekend. You can't expect too much in the way of practical progress today and so might as well concentrate on your social life, which looks better. A good time for forward looking personal plans.

28 FRIDAY

Moon Age Day 28 • Moon Sign Scorpio

am...

pm...
Enthusiasm is still on the wane and so there is little to do except to enjoy
the everyday events that unfold around you and to lay down the traces
of responsibility for a few hours. Don't try to disprove anything to anyone
or you could find that you are getting yourself in more hot water than if
you remained silent.

29 SATURDAY

Moon Age Day 0 • Moon Sign Scorpio

am...

pm...
A slightly testing time in one-to-one relationships and a period that
demands a fairly gentle touch on your behalf. This should not be too
difficult to achieve whilst you are in your present diplomatic frame of
mind. Meanwhile you can take a rest from the demands that have been
made of you professionally.

30 SUNDAY

Moon Age Day 1 • Moon Sign Sagittarius

am...

pm...
Avoid being over judgmental about the attitudes and the behaviour of
your friends right now. You could find further down the road that they
have reasons for behaving as they do that you cannot understand at
present. The end of the month may bring slightly better financial
prospects and greater contentment.

← NEGATIVE TREND							POSITIVE TREND →				
-5	-4	-3	-2	-1			+1	+2	+3	+4	+5
					LOVE						
					MONEY						
					LUCK						
					VITALITY						

1997

YOUR MONTH AT A GLANCE

The twelve numbered boxes represent the important areas in your life. The key to the numbers you will find beneath the panel. A sun above the number indicates that opportunities are around. A cloud below the number, that you should be a bit defensive. Nothing above or below and life will be pretty ordinary.

1	2	3	4	5	6	7	8	9	10	11	12

KEY

1 Strength of Personality
2 Personal Finance
3 Useful Information Gathering
4 Domestic Affairs
5 Pleasure & Romance
6 Effective Work & Health

7 One to One Relationships
8 Questioning, Thinking & Deciding
9 External Influences / Education
10 Career Aspirations
11 Teamwork Activities
12 Unconscious Impulses

DECEMBER HIGHS AND LOWS

Here, I show how the rhythm of the Moon will affect you this month. Like the tide, your energies and abilities will rise and fall with its pattern. When it is above the date line, go-for-it. When it is below the line you should be resting.

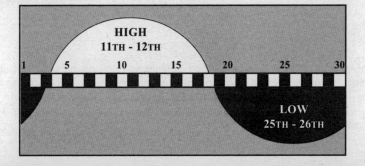

HIGH
11TH - 12TH

1   5   10   15   20   25   30

LOW
25TH - 26TH

1 MONDAY *Moon Age Day 2   Moon Sign Sagittarius*

am ....

pm ....
Mercury entering your solar ninth house represents something of an intellectual peak as far as you are concerned. It stimulates your ability to talk and makes it likely that you will press issues with others that normally you would want to leave alone. Someone you don't see too often turns up quite soon.

2 TUESDAY *Moon Age Day 3   Moon Sign Capricorn*

am ....

pm ....
No matter how exciting the prospects in a romantic sense, you should look at them very carefully before you get involved. Not everyone is entirely reliable and you should stay away from those individuals who you know to be disreputable. Taureans occasionally chase sensation, which is not sensible right now.

3 WEDNESDAY *Moon Age Day 4   Moon Sign Capricorn*

am ....

pm ....
Don't expect everything to be too secure at the moment because it won't be. Not that this means you are likely to have a dull or a difficult time, in fact nothing could be further from the truth. Interest comes from many different directions and centres very much on the attitude you have of yourself and your life.

4 THURSDAY *Moon Age Day 5   Moon Sign Aquarius*

am ....

pm ....
Professional issues have a part to play in your thinking today, if only because you are deciding on some new course of action or else taking the traces of life more firmly in your own hands than has been possible for a while now. Others see you as being quite powerful at the moment and it suits you to allow them to.

5 FRIDAY

Moon Age Day 6   Moon Sign Aquarius

am ....

pm ....
With your feet planted firmly on the ground, the really practical side of
Taurus now begins to show out much more. There are things that you
want in a material sense that are now much easier to command. Money
matters should be fairly settled and you are not likely to find any major
obstacles in your path.

6 SATURDAY

Moon Age Day 7   Moon Sign Aquarius

am ....

pm ....
If there are problems within your social circle it is not likely that they are
being created by you. Nevertheless you may be expected to sort them out
and can only really do so by becoming involved in situations that may not
be comfortable. Not that this will stop you because you want to create
peace now.

7 SUNDAY

Moon Age Day 8   Moon Sign Pisces

am ....

pm ....
Probably planning already for Christmas and fairly happy to spend the
day doing this and that, you should not expect a particularly dynamic
period to be coming along. You will never be far from excitement but
might find it difficult to get yourself right into the middle of it. Expectations can outstrip possibilities.

← NEGATIVE TREND						POSITIVE TREND →				
-5	-4	-3	-2	-1		+1	+2	+3	+4	+5
					LOVE					
					MONEY					
					LUCK					
					VITALITY					

8 MONDAY ♦ *Moon Age Day 9 • Moon Sign Pisces*

am ....

pm ....
There is no shortage of demands being made of you at present and there is nothing else for it but to get stuck in and to sort out as many of them as you can. There should still be plenty of time to please yourself however and the evening especially might seem as if it was made exclusively for you to enjoy.

9 TUESDAY ♦ *Moon Age Day 10 • Moon Sign Aries*

am ....

pm ....
This is a very good day and yet many of the benefits could come about as a result of the fact that other people are not seeing eye to eye. How this has a bearing on your life will become more clear in the fullness of time but you will need to keep your ears open and be prepared to make definite moves when necessary.

10 WEDNESDAY ♦ *Moon Age Day 11 • Moon Sign Aries*

am ....

pm ....
The best day of the month to put new ideas into action. You are intuitive and very practical at the same time. The combination of possibilities thrown up by present trends is especially important to you, not just at the moment but for a long time to come. Look well beyond Christmas and the New Year.

11 THURSDAY ♦ *Moon Age Day 12   Moon Sign Taurus*

am ....

pm ....
There are bound to be certain situations that you can take advantage of at this time and you do all you can to get on in life, both personally and in a material sense. Just be careful that you do not expect too much of yourself and balance work and play in equal amounts. Good friends are on hand at present.

12 FRIDAY ♦ *Moon Age Day 13 • Moon Sign Taurus*

am ....

pm ....
Today marks the last really lucky phase ahead of Christmas. This is not to suggest that the remainder of the month is especially dull, though it will be very busy and may not leave you the time to look at your own life that exists now. A good day to plan small events for later that will ensure your independence.

13 SATURDAY ♦ *Moon Age Day 14 • Moon Sign Gemini*

am ....

pm ....
There may be some prospect for improvements of a financial sort, even if they are slight and perhaps rather tenuous. Stay away from people who want to draw you into situations that you know can never do you any real good in the long run. Perhaps Taurus is just a little too suggestible for its own good today.

14 SUNDAY ♦ *Moon Age Day 15 • Moon Sign Gemini*

am ....

pm ....
Things that you have already done need to be undertaken again and you should find yourself in a good position to get them right this time round. You need to save a few hours during which you can please yourself, even if this means that you feel rather selfish. It is not an accusation that others would make.

← NEGATIVE TREND							POSITIVE TREND →			
-5	-4	-3	-2	-1		+1	+2	+3	+4	+5
					LOVE					
					MONEY					
					LUCK					
					VITALITY					

15 MONDAY   ♦   *Moon Age Day 16 • Moon Sign Cancer*

am . . . .

pm . . . .
It isn't always easy to discover that you have been doing something in
completely the wrong way, but if to do so allows you to put matters right
then the exercise is probably worthwhile. This is a strange day for
children of Venus, but that does not mean to say that it is devoid of any
gains.

16 TUESDAY   ♦   *Moon Age Day 17 • Moon Sign Cancer*

am . . . .

pm . . . .
When it comes to making important decisions you are going to have to
be especially careful today. It would be far too easy to say or do the wrong
thing and get yourself on the wrong side of people you need to rely on.
Being both bold and adventurous at the moment, it could be difficult to
find a happy medium.

17 WEDNESDAY   ♦   *Moon Age Day 18 • Moon Sign Leo*

am . . . .

pm . . . .
Domestic life could be the most rewarding area to deal with at present
and you are unlikely to be giving all that much to professional matters
just now. A careful appraisal of your financial situation may well be
called for and you might find yourself surprised by the prospect of more
money coming in.

18 THURSDAY   ♦   *Moon Age Day 19 • Moon Sign Leo*

am . . . .

pm . . . .
Now you feel yourself to be much wiser in the working area of life and will
not want to be held back by anyone at all. Give and take are important
in personal situations but that might not be all that easy at a time when
your nearest and dearest are so difficult to deal with. Maybe it is best to
retreat and wait.

19 FRIDAY ♦ *Moon Age Day 20 • Moon Sign Leo*

am...

pm...
A more boisterous Taurean is now on display and you will be doing all
that you can to make the most out of life and all that it is offering. Last
minute plans associated with Christmas are finally sorted out and you
should discover that there are offers about in a personal sense that you
cannot refuse.

20 SATURDAY ♦ *Moon Age Day 21 • Moon Sign Virgo*

am...

pm...
Those people you thought were trustworthy need looking at a little more
carefully at present. It is still best to retain an open mind about them
but at the same time your ideas and plans could be undermined if you
don't keep your eyes open. You are not exactly judgmental at the
moment, but are sensible.

21 SUNDAY ♦ *Moon Age Day 22 • Moon Sign Virgo*

am...

pm...
Venus is now strong in your solar tenth house. It is a planet that is
always of great importance to you, being your own natural ruler. You can
expect a favourable response from the people you have to deal with at all
levels, but particularly so in a personal sense. You home life should be
very settled.

← *NEGATIVE TREND*						*POSITIVE TREND* →				
-5	-4	-3	-2	-1		+1	+2	+3	+4	+5
					LOVE					
					MONEY					
					LUCK					
					VITALITY					

22 MONDAY ♦ *Moon Age Day 23 • Moon Sign Libra*

am ....

pm ....
You are now able to widen your horizons much more and you can thank
the changing position of the Sun in your chart for the fact. For a month
or so it should be much easier to assess others and to expect more of them.
Intuition is especially strong and is very unlikely to let you down.

23 TUESDAY ♦ *Moon Age Day 24 • Moon Sign Libra*

am ....

pm ....
There is a slight halt in some of the personal changes you have been
wanting to make, not least of all those relating to the onset of the festive
season. Even if you find that you have to change your mind at the last
minute there is no reason why the results should turn out to be less
successful than you hoped.

24 WEDNESDAY ♦ *Moon Age Day 25 • Moon Sign Libra*

am ....

pm ....
The lunar low comes along to slow things down a little on Christmas Eve.
It isn't that you have a particularly bad day, merely that it doesn't turn
out to be quite what you might have caused yourself to expect. This could
be because you have failed to be totally realistic and expect too much of
yourself.

25 THURSDAY ♦ *Moon Age Day 26 • Moon Sign Scorpio*

am ....

pm ....
It could well turn out to be a very family motivated sort of Christmas
Day, with plenty to enjoy and a feast of delight coming from the direction
of those you love. Friends will play a part too, though it is unlikely that
you would be moving away from your own fireside all that much more
than you have to.

26 FRIDAY ♦ *Moon Age Day 27 • Moon Sign Scorpio*

am..

pm..
A much more dynamic sort of day is forecast now and so Boxing day could mean a great deal more mixing and a much more elevated desire to be out and about in the world at large. Don't let general effort wane simply because you are in the middle of the holidays. There is nothing to prevent you from planning.

27 SATURDAY *Moon Age Day 28 • Moon Sign Sagittarius*

am..

pm..
For assertiveness and boldness you just cannot be bettered today and the bravery which is so much a part of your nature at the moment is likely to shine out as bright as the Sun. If you have to go journeying at the moment, be sure that you have sorted out all details as quickly as you are able to do.

28 SUNDAY *Moon Age Day 29 • Moon Sign Sagittarius*

am..

pm..
Expect the unexpected and then you won't be at all surprised by what today has to offer you. From dawn to dusk life is apt to throw all sorts of unusual possibilities in your path and you are willing to play the detective under most circumstances. Remember though that your curiosity has been known to get out of control.

← NEGATIVE TREND						POSITIVE TREND →				
-5	-4	-3	-2	-1		+1	+2	+3	+4	+5
					LOVE					
					MONEY					
					LUCK					
					VITALITY					

29 MONDAY
Moon Age Day 0 • Moon Sign Sagittarius

am..

pm..
Many of you will be back at work today and to be quite honest you have
probably had more than enough of holiday time in any case. It is a period
for getting yourself much more into gear and for feeling that, at last, life
is going more your way. In reality it has done so all along. You were
simply not watching!

30 TUESDAY
Moon Age Day 1 • Moon Sign Capricorn

am..

pm..
Any unexpected tiredness today is probably not so much of a surprise
after all. The truth is that you have been burning up a great deal of
nervous energy and that you may not have had the complete, mental and
physical rest, that is so important to you. Any arguments today should
be studiously avoided if possible.

31 WEDNESDAY
Moon Age Day 2 • Moon Sign Capricorn

am..

pm..
It's the last day of the year, and yet a brand new start as far as you are
concerned. Anxious as always to do what you know to be right, your are
less likely to be diverted from your path at this time. Gains come from
all sorts of directions and it is likely that your resolutions are sound and
eminently reasonable.

1 THURSDAY
Moon Age Day 3 • Moon Sign Aquarius

am..

pm..
Under no circumstances should be be willing to give in to negative trends
on the first day of the year. You can get through them, round them or over
them. It does not really matter which option you choose because in the
end you will be pleased with yourself that you stuck at it and got matters
sorted out.

2 FRIDAY

Moon Age Day 4 • Moon Sign Aquarius

am . . . .

pm . . . .
There is less reason to stand up for yourself today, mainly because others are managing to do it for you. Friends prove to be especially helpful and bring a new series of incentives into your life, staring right now. It already looks as though this year is going to be something really special.

3 SATURDAY

Moon Age Day 5 • Moon Sign Pisces

am . . . .

pm . . . .
Saturday appears to bring pause for thought, but not for long. The truth is that you are busy and determined to do everything that you can, all at the same time. Dare I tell you to slow down a bit? In all probability you will not take much notice, but at least you cannot say that you were not warned.

4 SUNDAY

Moon Age Day 6 • Moon Sign Pisces

am . . . .

pm . . . .
Defending others comes as second nature to you today, and this means that your loyalty will be repaid later on. A joke at the right time can defuse a potentially difficult situation and allows you to laugh at yourself too. Taureans are sometimes accused of being too serious. Prove that you are not.

← *NEGATIVE TREND*							*POSITIVE TREND* →			
-5	-4	-3	-2	-1		+1	+2	+3	+4	+5
					LOVE					
					MONEY					
					LUCK					
					VITALITY					

67

1998

YOUR MONTH AT A GLANCE

The twelve numbered boxes represent the important areas in your life. The key to the numbers you will find beneath the panel. A sun above the number indicates that opportunities are around. A cloud below the number, that you should be a bit defensive. Nothing above or below and life will be pretty ordinary.

1	2	3	4	5	6	7	8	9	10	11	12

KEY

1 Strength of Personality
2 Personal Finance
3 Useful Information Gathering
4 Domestic Affairs
5 Pleasure & Romance
6 Effective Work & Health

7 One to One Relationships
8 Questioning, Thinking & Deciding
9 External Influences / Education
10 Career Aspirations
11 Teamwork Activities
12 Unconscious Impulses

JANUARY HIGHS AND LOWS

Here, I show how the rhythm of the Moon will affect you this month. Like the tide, your energies and abilities will rise and fall with its pattern. When it is above the date line, go-for-it. When it is below the line you should be resting.

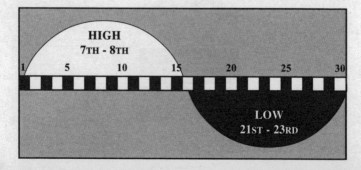

5 MONDAY
Moon Age Day 7 • Moon Sign Aries

am ....

pm ....
There are personal matters about that you really do want to get to the bottom of. Sometimes it is very useful to put your detective head on, just as long as you remember that not everything has a rational explanation. You should be able to rely on the help and support coming from friends.

6 TUESDAY
Moon Age Day 8 • Moon Sign Aries

am ....

pm ....
The pace of life tends to slow down a little now and you should find that you have quite a few moments to yourself. This does not mean that the pace of your thinking is altered, though it is likely that your more careful side is showing. Probably a good period for whispering words of love.

7 WEDNESDAY
Moon Age Day 9 • Moon Sign Taurus

am ....

pm ....
Along comes the lunar high and this represents the first of two days when every bit of effort that you put into life turns out to be more than worthwhile. Few people can beat you in a discussion now but this is not a good period for arguing simply for the sake of the exercise. Try to concentrate.

8 THURSDAY
Moon Age Day 10 • Moon Sign Taurus

am ....

pm ....
The Moon is still on your side and there is plenty to look forward to at this stage of the month. The attitude of your friends should be improving significantly and there are people around who prove reliable. Any financial decisions taken at this time should work out well for you.

9 FRIDAY
Moon Age Day 11 • Moon Sign Gemini

am ....

pm ....
It is likely that you will be very impatient in your dealings with those around you at this time and you need to look very carefully at your own attitude if you are not to offer offence. The truth is that you simply have to accept that not everyone agrees with your ideas at the present time.

10 SATURDAY
Moon Age Day 12 • Moon Sign Gemini

am ....

pm ....
It might prove to be a waste of time doing the same things over and over again. All the same you know your own nature best of all and if it is necessary to go over old ground then this is the way that you ought to proceed. Just make certain that you have thought things through first.

11 SUNDAY
Moon Age Day 13 • Moon Sign Gemini

am ....

pm ....
As far as your career is concerned you should now find that progress is much easier to make. Not everyone wants to follow you down a path that they may find too rocky for their own good. The truth is that you are more courageous at present than you are able to realise.

← *NEGATIVE TREND*   *POSITIVE TREND* →

-5	-4	-3	-2	-1		+1	+2	+3	+4	+5
					LOVE					
					MONEY					
					LUCK					
					VITALITY					

12 MONDAY   *Moon Age Day 14 • Moon Sign Cancer*

am ....

pm ....
Your curiosity is fired up at the start of the working week and it is likely that you are already planning to give at least part of the week to solving a mystery or dealing with a puzzling family matter. Loved ones should be only too willing to offer some timely assistance by this evening.

13 TUESDAY   *Moon Age Day 15 • Moon Sign Cancer*

am ....

pm ....
A family member is now likely to get the upper hand in a matter that you cannot control as you would wish. Of course there is no reason at all why you should have to make an issue out of the situation and you are only going to lose if you first consider that there is some kind of contest.

14 WEDNESDAY   *Moon Age Day 16 • Moon Sign Leo*

am ....

pm ....
Keep broadening your horizons. You can't go wrong if you stick to matters that you understand very well, though remain willing to look at them in a new way. You can gain from the positive way that friends are looking at you and from the things they are inclined to say as a result.

15 THURSDAY   *Moon Age Day 17 • Moon Sign Leo*

am ....

pm ....
Still generally decisive and well able to choose a path in life that really suits you, this is not a good period for doing the expected thing. Of course this really depends on whether you consider that routines are the best way to succeed. Chances are that you will opt for some real changes.

16 FRIDAY
Moon Age Day 18 • Moon Sign Virgo

am . . . .

pm . . . .
An excellent time for travel and for broadening your horizons, even if you can't get out and about. Cast your mind forward and towards new possibilities, and as at all stages this month, don't be afraid to speak your mind. You might be amazed at your own success just at present.

17 SATURDAY
Moon Age Day 19 • Moon Sign Virgo

am . . . .

pm . . . .
The full force of your personality tends to be on display today and you are good to know. If this means that your friends or colleagues want to make more of you, or rely on your judgement, it is only to be expected. You will not let them or yourself down now if you remain positive.

18 SUNDAY
Moon Age Day 20 • Moon Sign Virgo

am . . . .

pm . . . .
It may suddenly seem that there is one problem after another at work, though few of them will hold you up for any length of time. Your own personal attitude has a great deal to do with situation and so it would be best to try and maintain the generally positive attitude of recent days.

← NEGATIVE TREND							POSITIVE TREND →				
-5	-4	-3	-2	-1			+1	+2	+3	+4	+5
					LOVE						
					MONEY						
					LUCK						
					VITALITY						

19 MONDAY
Moon Age Day 21 • Moon Sign Libra

am ....

pm ....
You may be intensely curious about certain matters at this time and will find it necessary to turn over any stone in your search for the truth. This is fine, as long as you remember that there are certain matters that have no solution, or at least not one that would make any real sense.

20 TUESDAY
Moon Age Day 22 • Moon Sign Libra

am ....

pm ....
It might be all too easy to upset those people who you are going to have to rely on in the not too distant future. All the more reason to tread carefully at present and to stay close to matters that are not contentious. Create a happy atmosphere as far as home life is concerned.

21 WEDNESDAY
Moon Age Day 23 • Moon Sign Scorpio

am ....

pm ....
You are winning through again, even in those areas where you have been rather stuck during the last couple of days. It might be difficult to make the sort of practical progress that you would wish, because the lunar low tends to get in the way. Problems are not going to last however.

22 THURSDAY
Moon Age Day 24 • Moon Sign Scorpio

am ....

pm ....
It is in the area of personal relationships where you could find the position of the Moon to be something of a problem today. It would certainly be wise not to push your point of view too much, since by doing so you could be digging yourself into a hole that takes time to get out of.

23 FRIDAY

Moon Age Day 25 • Moon Sign Scorpio

am..

pm..
Relationships are likely to feel anything but secure at this time, and you need to tread very carefully if you are not to get on the wrong side of people who you usually can rely on. As creative as your sign is inclined to be, this might be a good time for home decorating or some other project.

24 SATURDAY

Moon Age Day 26 • Moon Sign Sagittarius

am..

pm..
The tables turn and now you find that any social situation suits you down to the ground. Be bold and certain when you are dealing with new individuals and show them right from the start just how positive you are capable of being. A general improvement financially seems to be coming.

25 SUNDAY

Moon Age Day 27 • Moon Sign Sagittarius

am..

pm..
Toeing the line with others in any situation just does not suit you at the moment, and especially so since life is teaming you up with people who prove determined to get your back up in the first place. Activity of any sort might take your mind off more mundane problems that beset you.

← *NEGATIVE TREND*							*POSITIVE TREND* →				
-5	-4	-3	-2	-1		+1	+2	+3	+4	+5
					LOVE					
					MONEY					
					LUCK					
					VITALITY					

26 MONDAY
Moon Age Day 28 • Moon Sign Capricorn

am..

pm..
Freedom is the key to personal success, both today and until the end of the month. Realising that what you achieve is more or less down to the effort that you are willing to put in, you may be inclined to rush your fences too much. Slow and steady wins practical races just at present.

27 TUESDAY
Moon Age Day 29 • Moon Sign Capricorn

am..

pm..
You should find that you have certain advantages over others today, and especially so when it comes to your personal drive for freedom. Probably not a good time for staying too close to home. The truth is that you tend to be rather restless and inclined to feel hemmed in by circumstance.

28 WEDNESDAY
Moon Age Day 0 • Moon Sign Aquarius

am..

pm..
Expect the unexpected today and you probably cannot go wrong. There are certainly some surprises in store, though it would be safe to suggest that the majority of them work very much in your favour. Routines are still likely to get on your nerves, even very necessary ones.

29 THURSDAY
Moon Age Day 1 • Moon Sign Aquarius

am..

pm..
Counting on others is not too easy at this stage of the working week and there is a real possibility that you will have to go it alone. Try to avoid allowing yourself to get down in the mouth about issues that it is not possible for you to control and concentrate on matters you can solve.

30 FRIDAY

Moon Age Day 2 • Moon Sign Pisces

am...

pm...
A positive light shines on any group venture that you find yourself
involved in at this time. There are certain distractions to deal with,
though as long as you keep your temper you should even be able to turn
these round to your own unique point of view. Others really want to help.

31 SATURDAY

Moon Age Day 3 • Moon Sign Pisces

am...

pm...
Intellectual debates are all very well, but do they get the washing done?
The simple fact is that your more practical Taurean attributes are the
best ones to rely on at present, even when your nearest and dearest are
running round like headless chickens. Try to understand their attitude
too though.

1 SUNDAY

Moon Age Day 4 • Moon Sign Aries

am...

pm...
Don't allow yourself to be drawn back into the past since this is a
destination that will do you no good at all just at the present time. The
most important fact right now is that you feel you are making progress,
which you cannot do if you are time travelling in the wrong direction
entirely.

← NEGATIVE TREND						POSITIVE TREND →				
-5	-4	-3	-2	-1		+1	+2	+3	+4	+5
					LOVE					
					MONEY					
					LUCK					
					VITALITY					

1998

YOUR MONTH AT A GLANCE

The twelve numbered boxes represent the important areas in your life. The key to the numbers you will find beneath the panel. A sun above the number indicates that opportunities are around. A cloud below the number, that you should be a bit defensive. Nothing above or below and life will be pretty ordinary.

| 1 | 2 | 3 | 4 | 5 | 6 | 7 | 8 | 9 | 10 | 11 | 12 |

KEY

1 Strength of Personality
2 Personal Finance
3 Useful Information Gathering
4 Domestic Affairs
5 Pleasure & Romance
6 Effective Work & Health

7 One to One Relationships
8 Questioning, Thinking & Deciding
9 External Influences / Education
10 Career Aspirations
11 Teamwork Activities
12 Unconscious Impulses

FEBRUARY HIGHS AND LOWS

Here, I show how the rhythm of the Moon will affect you this month. Like the tide, your energies and abilities will rise and fall with its pattern. When it is above the date line, go-for-it. When it is below the line you should be resting.

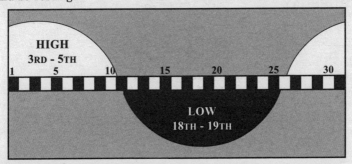

HIGH
3RD - 5TH

LOW
18TH - 19TH

2 MONDAY

Moon Age Day 5 • Moon Sign Aries

am..

pm..
The idealistic side of your nature shines out at present, probably rather
more than is good for you. There are gains to be made at a practical and
financial level, but they might be missed if you spend too much time
thinking about ethics. You can always be charitable a little later.

3 TUESDAY

Moon Age Day 6 • Moon Sign Taurus

am..

pm..
With the Moon favourably placed to allow you two days of real progress,
you first need to decide what is most important for the moment. If you
have to work, make certain that you put your ideas across to those of
influence. Should you be at home, talk to family members.

4 WEDNESDAY

Moon Age Day 7 • Moon Sign Taurus

am..

pm..
You could find that you have a significant amount of energy to spare,
even though there might not be quite as much to do with it as you would
wish. Try to curb your enthusiasm a little because life itself offers you
all the incentives you could possibly need. Not a time to interfere.

5 THURSDAY

Moon Age Day 8 • Moon Sign Taurus

am..

pm..
It's possible that you are feeling like a fish out of water, especially at
work. If this does turn out to be the case try to find a little space to be
yourself and leave some of the more practical aspects of life until a little
later. By the evening you should be back on top form once again.

6 FRIDAY   *Moon Age Day 9 • Moon Sign Gemini*

am ....

pm ....
Material matters and ways of making money seem to be at the top of your
agenda just at present and you should find many ways in which to better
yourself as the day advances. With a great deal of support possible from
some fairly forward looking and influential types life appears good.

7 SATURDAY   *Moon Age Day 10 • Moon Sign Gemini*

am ....

pm ....
Although it isn't usually the case, at the present time you are inclined to
change your mind about things all too easily. For this reason it would
be better to delay important decisions until tomorrow. In the meantime
you can concentrate instead on having a good time personally.

8 SUNDAY   *Moon Age Day 11 • Moon Sign Cancer*

am ....

pm ....
An ideal time to go with the flow, which is probably travelling very much
in your direction of its own accord. You could be quite surprised if you
don't have to put any effort into life. Simply make the best of present
trends and take what is on offer from life as a gift to you personally.

← NEGATIVE TREND						POSITIVE TREND →				
-5	-4	-3	-2	-1		+1	+2	+3	+4	+5
					LOVE	▓				
					MONEY	▓	▓			
					LUCK	▓				
				▓	VITALITY					

9 MONDAY
Moon Age Day 12 • Moon Sign Cancer

am . . . .

pm . . . .
Some Taureans are going to be a little irritable today. If you are one of them you can at least be sure that this trend is not going to last very long. Should things get really bad all you can do is to stay out of the way of people who you really do not want to upset at this important time.

10 TUESDAY
Moon Age Day 13 • Moon Sign Leo

am . . . .

pm . . . .
The focus today seems to be very much on family life, which is probably not all that surprising considering present trends. There are any number of ways to make yourself happy but you will not want to push any personal issue too hard at the present time. Let situations mature before pushing them.

11 WEDNESDAY
Moon Age Day 14 • Moon Sign Leo

am . . . .

pm . . . .
Keep your eyes and ears open for new and stimulating experiences now. With a more go ahead attitude and plenty to play for in the financial stakes, you should also find that your general level of good luck is on the increase. A time to take the bull by the horns regarding romance.

12 THURSDAY
Moon Age Day 15 • Moon Sign Leo

am . . . .

pm . . . .
An association between Mercury and Saturn today allows you the chance to 'ground' some of the sort of plans that have been rather flighty until now. Prepare yourself for a more interesting and eventful interlude and make certain you don't hang back when an answer is required.

13 FRIDAY

Moon Age Day 16 • Moon Sign Virgo

am ....

pm ....

An excellent day for creative activities and for making your mind up about a possible change of circumstances at work. Although you may be rather hesitant when it comes to speaking your mind in a personal sense, it appears as though you are approaching a more dominant phase now.

14 SATURDAY

Moon Age Day 17 • Moon Sign Virgo

am ....

pm ....

You might be in two minds about a professional situation and the part it is going to play in your life during the weeks ahead. If you have thought things through carefully in the recent past there is no point in constantly jumping from one foot to the other. Have confidence in yourself.

15 SUNDAY

Moon Age Day 18 • Moon Sign Libra

am ....

pm ....

The Sun in your solar tenth house now acts as another incentive to get things moving in almost any way that takes your fancy. There are people around whom you will find to be of great interest, and especially so when it comes to leisure activities. A day to speak your mind personally.

← NEGATIVE TREND						POSITIVE TREND →				
-5	-4	-3	-2	-1	LOVE	+1	+2	+3	+4	+5
					MONEY					
					LUCK					
					VITALITY					

16 MONDAY

Moon Age Day 19 • Moon Sign Libra

am...

pm...
You should be very happy at the start of this working week to get on with
the task in hand in your own careful and considered way. The bearing
that other people have on you should be fairly limited at present, which
will not worry you but might have a part to play in their attitude.

17 TUESDAY

Moon Age Day 20 • Moon Sign Libra

am...

pm...
The Moon is in your opposite sign later and that means that you might
feel that certain aspects of life are proving to be less than helpful. Treat
this as a thinking time and you probably cannot put a foot wrong.
Probably not a good time for chancing your arm or for making too much
of situations.

18 WEDNESDAY

Moon Age Day 21 • Moon Sign Scorpio

am...

pm...
With less apparent personal influence whilst the lunar low is about, you
have to realise that what you are going through at the moment is nothing
more than a short interlude. As long as you realise that more difficult
trends will pass they have little chance of stopping your forward
progress.

19 THURSDAY

Moon Age Day 22 • Moon Sign Scorpio

am...

pm...
The Moon starts to move on, but not before it imposes one or two slight
reversals upon you. Look at such matters carefully because it is very
likely that you can turn almost any situation to your advantage if you
only think about it for a while. A good day for speaking words of love.

20 FRIDAY
Moon Age Day 23 • Moon Sign Sagittarius

am . . . .

pm . . . .
With the Sun now changing position in your chart you should find this
to be the start of a period when you can take full advantage of the many
personal ambitions that are within you. For the next month or so dreams
represent the start of positive actions that go towards making fantasy
into reality.

21 SATURDAY
Moon Age Day 24 • Moon Sign Sagittarius

am . . . .

pm . . . .
Be prepared to change some very important plans, almost at a moment's
notice if you must. Not a time for standing still but for showing the world
what you are really made of . Creative activities may have to wait for a
while but it isn't long before you are back in gear in this respect too.

22 SUNDAY
Moon Age Day 25 • Moon Sign Capricorn

am . . . .

pm . . . .
Group activities and associations of people become more interesting and
more lucrative in the days ahead. You may be biting at the bit regarding
a personal ambition or a discovery that is of great importance to you at
this time. Of course patience is a virtue that you were born to possess.

← *NEGATIVE TREND*						*POSITIVE TREND* →				
-5	-4	-3	-2	-1		+1	+2	+3	+4	+5
					LOVE					
					MONEY					
					LUCK					
					VITALITY					

23 MONDAY
Moon Age Day 26 • Moon Sign Capricorn

am...

pm...
Whilst you are clearly full of positive ideas at the moment, putting some of them into practice is not going to be all that easy. All the more reason to take a day out during which you can more or less please yourself and during which you can mull over plans that are going to take some time.

24 TUESDAY
Moon Age Day 27 • Moon Sign Capricorn

am...

pm...
Most Taureans should be on top form today and there should be very little that has the power to hold you back. Friends and relatives line up to lend a hand when it is necessary for them to do so and you manage to line up potentials in an order that makes them very easy to deal with.

25 WEDNESDAY
Moon Age Day 28 • Moon Sign Aquarius

am...

pm...
If there are any slight niggles in your mind this is the time to bring them to the surface. Of course you cannot expect that everyone truly understands what you are talking about, though if you talk quietly and explain yourself carefully, you could be surprised at the positive results that come along.

26 THURSDAY
Moon Age Day 0 • Moon Sign Aquarius

am...

pm...
Teamwork really counts at the moment and this turns out to be a key day, not only for you, but probably for anyone with whom you have contact. Your friends prove to be especially loyal at the present time and will back you up, even on the odd occasions when they know you are wrong.

27 FRIDAY   *Moon Age Day 1 • Moon Sign Pisces*

am ....

pm ....
Love life and relationships might have been just a little neglected of late
and today represents and ideal interlude for putting them right. Take
some moments out to talk to your lover or to family members. There is
much that can be said, and you now have all the tact necessary to speak
out.

28 SATURDAY   *Moon Age Day 2 • Moon Sign Pisces*

am ....

pm ....
Sit back and take stock of current affairs. Life should be going more or
less the way that you would wish and it is only a matter of time before
the effort you have been putting in begins to pay some fairly handsome
dividends. Act with certainty when it comes to dealing with family
matters.

1 SUNDAY   *Moon Age Day 3 • Moon Sign Aries*

am ....

pm ....
Some very good Venusian influences are likely to enhance certain areas
of your love life and offer you a great deal of certainty in your dealings
with those people who are the most important to you at present. Don't
be too surprised if some compliments are coming your way later.

← NEGATIVE TREND							POSITIVE TREND →			
-5	-4	-3	-2	-1		+1	+2	+3	+4	+5
					LOVE					
					MONEY					
					LUCK					
					VITALITY					

1998

YOUR MONTH AT A GLANCE

The twelve numbered boxes represent the important areas in your life. The key to the numbers you will find beneath the panel. A sun above the number indicates that opportunities are around. A cloud below the number, that you should be a bit defensive. Nothing above or below and life will be pretty ordinary.

1	2	3	4	5	6	7	8	9	10	11	12

KEY

1 Strength of Personality
2 Personal Finance
3 Useful Information Gathering
4 Domestic Affairs
5 Pleasure & Romance
6 Effective Work & Health

7 One to One Relationships
8 Questioning, Thinking & Deciding
9 External Influences / Education
10 Career Aspirations
11 Teamwork Activities
12 Unconscious Impulses

MARCH HIGHS AND LOWS

Here, I show how the rhythm of the Moon will affect you this month. Like the tide, your energies and abilities will rise and fall with its pattern. When it is above the date line, go-for-it. When it is below the line you should be resting.

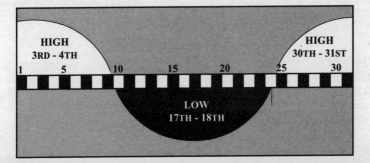

HIGH
3RD - 4TH

HIGH
30TH - 31ST

1   5   10   15   20   25   30

LOW
17TH - 18TH

2 MONDAY
Moon Age Day 4 • Moon Sign Aries

am ....

pm ....
Before the end of today you will be noticing the arrival of the lunar high. With everything to play for you need to make the most of circumstances by putting one or two plans into action now. Things will mature during the week and the signposts generally look especially positive.

3 TUESDAY
Moon Age Day 5 • Moon Sign Taurus

am ....

pm ....
If you are away from work for any reason today, you find yourself in a position to please yourself and to bring a good deal of fun into the lives of others at the same time. You are at your bright and breezy best, able to come to terms with necessary changes and anxious to get out and about.

4 WEDNESDAY
Moon Age Day 6 • Moon Sign Taurus

am ....

pm ....
Keep your eyes and ears open today and don't allow yourself to be pushed into any situation that is not of your own making. Creative and happy you should find this to be a Wednesday to remember, if only because there is time to do more or less whatever takes your personal fancy.

5 THURSDAY
Moon Age Day 7 • Moon Sign Gemini

am ....

pm ....
A new and possibly lucky trend comes along, thanks to the intervention of the planet Venus into your life. Personal relationships should be looking up and especially those of Taureans who have been a little down in the mouth concerning prospects for love and marriage in the near future.

6 FRIDAY
Moon Age Day 8 • Moon Sign Gemini

am..

pm..
Some of the efforts you have been making to assert yourself have been going mysteriously wrong in the last few days. You can be sure that these trends are now passing and that means that others are taking far more notice of you. Probably the best time of all for putting plans forward.

7 SATURDAY
Moon Age Day 9 • Moon Sign Cancer

am..

pm..
Pace yourself a little now that you are near the end of the week. There is little to be gained by rushing your fences and everything to be achieved from simply waiting and watching. Not everyone seems equally keen to fall in line with your propositions but it's only a matter of time before they do.

8 SUNDAY
Moon Age Day 10 • Moon Sign Cancer

am..

pm..
Matters requiring a higher degree of logic than has been available to you in the recent past now see you turning your mind in a more practical direction. With your feet firmly planted on the ground this is the time to make more of yourself, and for considering financial transactions.

← NEGATIVE TREND						POSITIVE TREND →				
-5	-4	-3	-2	-1		+1	+2	+3	+4	+5
					LOVE					
					MONEY					
					LUCK					
					VITALITY					

9 MONDAY

Moon Age Day 11 • Moon Sign Leo

am ....

pm ....
It will be much easier today to see who really does have your best
interests at heart and you are unlikely to have the wool pulled over your
eyes by anyone. Once you have made up your mind who you can trust,
it might be the right time for imparting a secret or two. Keep some things
to yourself though.

10 TUESDAY

Moon Age Day 12 • Moon Sign Leo

am ....

pm ....
You can put real charm to use right now when it comes to convincing
other people that you know what you are talking about. This technique
will work far better than trying to push your ideas forward like a steam
roller and you should discover that there is little to loose by speaking out.

11 WEDNESDAY

Moon Age Day 13 • Moon Sign Leo

am ....

pm ....
If it seems today as if you really do not belong in a centre stage position
do be willing to sit in the wings of life for a day or two. There is a very
quiet side to your nature that is obvious to everyone now and again and
half your appeal lies in smiling enigmatically when you know you are
right.

12 THURSDAY

Moon Age Day 14 • Moon Sign Virgo

am ....

pm ....
Avoid minor mishaps that are brought about as a result of hasty actions.
It would be far better to do any job more than once, if that is what it takes
to get things working properly, rather than to rush now and suffer later.
This fact is also true of friends, who you are in a position to advise.

13 FRIDAY
Moon Age Day 15 • Moon Sign Virgo

am. . . . .

pm. . . . .
Now more ingenious, you tend to take any task in your stride much more
readily and should find situations turning your way a great deal more
easily than at any stage during the last week. Possibilities are building
up at this stage and you have all the resources for greater success.

14 SATURDAY
Moon Age Day 16 • Moon Sign Libra

am. . . . .

pm. . . . .
Much less concerned with ambitions now, you tend to take life in your
stride and should find that the generally good trends are continuing as
a result. Seek out a pleasant space where you can be alone for an hour
or two whilst you think matters through carefully. A relaxed and happy
interlude.

15 SUNDAY
Moon Age Day 17 • Moon Sign Libra

am. . . . .

pm. . . . .
The favourable results you achieve from past practical application can
come as something of a surprise to you. Make no bones about it though,
this is all as a result of what you have laboured away at previously. If
any real gains come your way you can be certain that you deserve them.

← *NEGATIVE TREND*							*POSITIVE TREND* →				
-5	-4	-3	-2	-1		+1	+2	+3	+4	+5
					LOVE					
					MONEY					
					LUCK					
					VITALITY					

16 MONDAY

Moon Age Day 18 • Moon Sign Libra

am ....

pm ....
With the lunar low now showing its fact you are going to have to come
to terms with a slower pace of life and less in the way of material success
for a day or two. In a way this might turn out to be a good thing since
you now have the chance to sit and take stock of many elements of life.

17 TUESDAY

Moon Age Day 19 • Moon Sign Scorpio

am ....

pm ....
Let your partner or a good friend handle something which you would
normally want to deal with yourself. The Moon is still not in a startling
position for you and it would be all too easy to throw a spanner in the
works of something that you have laboured long and hard to bring to
fruition.

18 WEDNESDAY

Moon Age Day 20 • Moon Sign Scorpio

am ....

pm ....
The Moon begins to move away from your opposite sign, and though you
cannot expect to be on top form, today should prove to be positive enough
if you allow the chance to be so. Ideas can run ahead of you however and
it might be necessary to put the brakes on one or two of them for now.

19 THURSDAY

Moon Age Day 21 • Moon Sign Sagittarius

am ....

pm ....
The things that certain people in your vicinity are saying to you at
present tend to go over your head. This isn't because you lack intelli-
gence but is merely an interlude. Simply bear in mind what they are
saying and think about it for a day or two. All should become clear in the
end.

20 FRIDAY
Moon Age Day 22 • Moon Sign Sagittarius

am . . . .

pm . . . .
As the Sun alters your solar twelfth house so you find a new period opening when it appears you have a little less power to influence the world around you. In fact the reverse is true because you are also becoming much more perceptive. A happy conclusions to an old situation is likely.

21 SATURDAY
Moon Age Day 23 • Moon Sign Sagittarius

am . . . .

pm . . . .
Don't try to spread yourself too thinly at the moment because you are certain to come unstuck if you do. Allow yourself a little interlude during which you can choose for yourself but in the main remain true to one or two ideas only. The more you watch and wait the better things will be.

22 SUNDAY
Moon Age Day 24 • Moon Sign Capricorn

am . . . .

pm . . . .
A lucky interlude comes your way, thanks once again to the present position of the planet Venus. A good time to push your luck at work and for any limited form of speculation. Don't underestimate the power that friends have to bring situations full circle for you now.

← NEGATIVE TREND						POSITIVE TREND →				
-5	-4	-3	-2	-1		+1	+2	+3	+4	+5
					LOVE					
					MONEY					
					LUCK					
					VITALITY					

23 MONDAY   *Moon Age Day 25 • Moon Sign Capricorn*

am...

pm...
An issue from the past begins to show itself again now. Anyone who is responsible for watching your progress at work is likely to be taking notice of you now and so you would do well to be on your best behaviour. Concern for the underdog is inclined to hold you back somewhat.

24 TUESDAY   *Moon Age Day 26 • Moon Sign Aquarius*

am...

pm...
Much goodwill comes your way at present, and some of it from the least likely directions. Keep an open mind about possible changes to your home routines and don't allow yourself to be pushed into doing things that really do go against the grain. Taurean patience pays of now.

25 WEDNESDAY   *Moon Age Day 27 • Moon Sign Aquarius*

am...

pm...
When it comes to your own achievements in life you tend to keep a sense of proportion as a rule, though this may not be the case at the moment. The truth is that you are probably aiming for the stars. As long as you are willing to settle for a little less, all should turn out well in the long run.

26 THURSDAY   *Moon Age Day 28 • Moon Sign Pisces*

am...

pm...
Just remember that it is not possible for you to please everyone all the time, no matter how much you would wish to do so. This fact is of paramount importance to your general progress right now, since you are inclined to want the whole world to be happy. This is not possible.

27 FRIDAY

Moon Age Day 29 • Moon Sign Pisces

am . . . .

pm . . . .

Not a particularly good day for grandiose schemes, which quite frankly need to be kept firmly on the back burner just at present. If there is something that you have been particularly looking forward to in a personal sense, keep your eye on that possibility and let other matters wait in line.

28 SATURDAY ♦

Moon Age Day 0 • Moon Sign Aries

am . . . .

pm . . . .

You are very susceptible to the influence of others now, and particularly those from people who you find to be especially attractive. Remember though that all that glistens is not gold. This is especially true of Taurean relationships at present. As a result some care is necessary for now.

29 SUNDAY ♦

Moon Age Day 1 • Moon Sign Aries

am . . . .

pm . . . .

The spirit of harmony and co-operation that is possible now knows no bounds, even if the day as a whole appears to be quite quiet and less than eventful. Not all people have your best interests at heart but most do. Plan ahead now because very positive trends are in store soon.

← NEGATIVE TREND						POSITIVE TREND →				
-5	-4	-3	-2	-1		+1	+2	+3	+4	+5
					LOVE					
					MONEY					
					LUCK					
					VITALITY					

30 MONDAY ♦ *Moon Age Day 2 • Moon Sign Taurus*

am ....

pm ....

Lady Luck is about to pay you a visit, and this fact is much strengthened now that the Moon is back in your zodiac sign of Taurus. With everything to play for, financially and personally, it looks as though you cannot put a foot wrong. At work you could do worse than simply going with the flow.

31 TUESDAY ♦ *Moon Age Day 3 • Moon Sign Taurus*

am ....

pm ....

Keep the pressure on and work towards your objectives with a level of energy that knows no bounds at present. You will not want to be dashing about from pillar to post if there is a quicker way to get things done and enrolling the support of others seems the best way to go about things.

1 WEDNESDAY ♦ *Moon Age Day 4 • Moon Sign Gemini*

am ....

pm ....

You could find a little tension coming into your life today, which is all the more reason to stand back and look at things carefully. You are inclined by nature to proceed with caution and there has never been a better time for doing so. You do tend to be especially friendly at present.

2 THURSDAY ♦ *Moon Age Day 5 • Moon Sign Gemini*

am ....

pm ....

There are probably some minor disturbances to deal with at work, though it is not likely that these would hold you up for any length of time. Attitude is very important, especially when you are dealing with people who probably do not understand you particularly well.

3 FRIDAY   ♦   *Moon Age Day 6 • Moon Sign Cancer*

am . . . .

pm . . . .
Push yourself to the forefront a little more. There is likely to be a
situation that demands your specific attention but if you stay at the back
of the queue you may not even be asked for your opinion. A good day for
coming to terms with facts from the past as they bear on your life now.

4 SATURDAY   ♦   *Moon Age Day 7 • Moon Sign Cancer*

am . . . .

pm . . . .
Emotional impulses tend to drive you along at the moment and this is a
time when you need to be sure of your personal feelings before you are
prepared to speak out about them. Love comes knocking at your door in
more than one way and relatives set out to be very kind to you.

5 SUNDAY   ♦   *Moon Age Day 8 • Moon Sign Cancer*

am . . . .

pm . . . .
Professional matters start to go with a swing and especially so if you
make certain that you are in the right place at the correct time. What
you are saying an doing, even in a casual sense, can have a great part to
play in the way that you are appreciated by those around you for the next
few days.

← NEGATIVE TREND							POSITIVE TREND →				
-5	-4	-3	-2	-1			+1	+2	+3	+4	+5
					LOVE						
					MONEY						
					LUCK						
					VITALITY						

1998

YOUR MONTH AT A GLANCE

The twelve numbered boxes represent the important areas in your life. The key to the numbers you will find beneath the panel. A sun above the number indicates that opportunities are around. A cloud below the number, that you should be a bit defensive. Nothing above or below and life will be pretty ordinary.

1	2	3	4	5	6	7	8	9	10	11	12

KEY

1 Strength of Personality	7 One to One Relationships
2 Personal Finance	8 Questioning, Thinking & Deciding
3 Useful Information Gathering	9 External Influences / Education
4 Domestic Affairs	10 Career Aspirations
5 Pleasure & Romance	11 Teamwork Activities
6 Effective Work & Health	12 Unconscious Impulses

APRIL HIGHS AND LOWS

Here, I show how the rhythm of the Moon will affect you this month. Like the tide, your energies and abilities will rise and fall with its pattern. When it is above the date line, go-for-it. When it is below the line you should be resting.

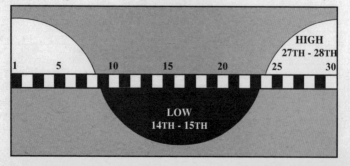

6 MONDAY ♦ *Moon Age Day 9 • Moon Sign Leo*

am ....

pm ....
Don't expect some matters to run quite as smoothly as you might wish.
If there are minor difficulties about, you tend to take them more or less
in your stride. Guessing games with friends probably ought to be avoided
since your usual patience is taking a short holiday right now.

7 TUESDAY ♦ *Moon Age Day 10 • Moon Sign Leo*

am ....

pm ....
Nostalgia plays a part in your life at present and it is likely that you are
looking back at a time that appears now to have been especially happy.
However, you are failing to register the things that went wrong then and
are probably a great deal better off thinking about the present.

8 WEDNESDAY ♦ *Moon Age Day 11 • Moon Sign Virgo*

am ....

pm ....
You are out there in the social mainstream of life and quite prepared to
do whatever it takes to push yourself and your ideas to the forefront.
Confidence is fairly high and you appear to know exactly what you want
from life, even if actually getting it somewhat more of a problem.

9 THURSDAY ♦ *Moon Age Day 12 • Moon Sign Virgo*

am ....

pm ....
Your desire to be friendly to one and all seems to be written all over your
face. Not that every single person you meet is going to take especially
kindly to this attitude and you might even have to talk one or two people
round to seeing things the way they appear in your personal universe.

10 FRIDAY ♦ *Moon Age Day 13 • Moon Sign Virgo*

am ....

pm ....
Powerful emotions rise to the surface at this time and it is difficult to be the steady and cool Taurean that many people recognise as a rule. It won't do the world any harm at all to realise that you are capable of deep and abiding feelings, even if some people are a little surprised by the fact.

11 SATURDAY ♦ *Moon Age Day 14 • Moon Sign Libra*

am ....

pm ....
A plan of action should be showing excellent signs of succeeding today so it is a case of getting stuck in and doing what you know personally to be right. Energy is not at all hard to find, and you are able to see old problems in a new and much more positive light for a day or two.

12 SUNDAY ♦ *Moon Age Day 15 • Moon Sign Libra*

am ....

pm ....
Although today probably brings only a minor peak in achievement, you should not underestimate the bearing that this will have on matters in the longer term. Crave the attention of someone who works close to you because if you combine your ideas with theirs, success is likely.

← NEGATIVE TREND						POSITIVE TREND →				
-5	-4	-3	-2	-1		+1	+2	+3	+4	+5
					LOVE					
					MONEY					
					LUCK					
					VITALITY					

13 MONDAY   ◆   *Moon Age Day 16 • Moon Sign Scorpio*

am ....

pm ....
Energy is in fairly short supply now that the Moon occupies your opposite
sign. For this reason you cannot expect the most dynamic start to the
working week. It would be sensible to allow others to take a little of the
strain at present, whilst you sit and think things through rather
carefully.

14 TUESDAY   ◆   *Moon Age Day 17 • Moon Sign Scorpio*

am ....

pm ....
A stay at home sort of time is likely and all the more so because of the
present position of the Moon. Creative potential is good and you might
be looking around yourself at the decor of your home, deciding that the
time is right to make some sort of alteration ahead of the summer
months.

15 WEDNESDAY   ◆   *Moon Age Day 18 • Moon Sign Scorpio*

am ....

pm ....
Some interesting proposals seem to be coming your way and aspects
indicate that it is likely that they come either from friends or family
members. If your mind keeps drifting back to the past, at least there are
present happenings to direct it forwards again. Love looks very good.

16 THURSDAY   ◆   *Moon Age Day 19 • Moon Sign Sagittarius*

am ....

pm ....
Much contentment and emotional fulfilment seems to be on the cards for
Taurus during this part of this working week. You feel yourself to be the
centre of attention in some way and have the ability to bask in the glow
of a very real affection that plays around you at work and at home.

17 FRIDAY
♦ *Moon Age Day 20 • Moon Sign Sagittarius*

am...

pm...
For a few small astrological reasons it is possible today that you will want
to shut the world out altogether and rest somewhat within your own
world. In some ways this would not be a bad thing, though you must not
forget that there are responsibilities to be dealt with at some stage.

18 SATURDAY
♦ *Moon Age Day 21 • Moon Sign Capricorn*

am...

pm...
Freedom is something that you never stop searching for, even if you tend
to conduct the search in a fairly low key sort of way. People seem
reasonable enough and if you have any complaints they are difficult to
quantify. You can't expect to be truly contented every moment of each
day.

19 SUNDAY
♦ *Moon Age Day 22 • Moon Sign Capricorn*

am...

pm...
A boost to your energy seems to be on the way, and not before time in the
case of some Taureans. Now you can really get yourself fully back into
harness and begin to express yourself in no uncertain terms. In personal
discussions a few words now tend to go a very long way.

← NEGATIVE TREND						POSITIVE TREND →				
-5	-4	-3	-2	-1		+1	+2	+3	+4	+5
					LOVE					
					MONEY					
					LUCK					
					VITALITY					

20 MONDAY   *Moon Age Day 23 • Moon Sign Aquarius*

am...

pm...
Minor obstructions of a professional nature might appear to be getting in your way at the start of today, that is until you realise that you can turn even these round to your own advantage. Whatever is asked of you, it tends to be easy for you to plan your strategy and make positive statements about it.

21 TUESDAY   *Moon Age Day 24 • Moon Sign Aquarius*

am...

pm...
Get ready to move as the tide of life takes on a new pace. There is everything to play for today, even if some of it does not seem to be of an entirely practical nature. Routines could get in the way at first, though only if you refuse to leave them alone, at least for the duration of today.

22 WEDNESDAY   *Moon Age Day 25 • Moon Sign Aquarius*

am...

pm...
There could be a little confusion regarding a career matter and this will have to thought out ahead of next week. At the same time you can save at least an hour or two for yourself and might arrive at a personal plan that is certain to bring an interesting new series of possibilities to bear on you.

23 THURSDAY   *Moon Age Day 26 • Moon Sign Pisces*

am...

pm...
Friends and associates are inclined to bring out the very best in you at this stage of the working week. With everything to play for it is likely that you will be up with the lark and raring to go. Stopping around to explain yourself to others does not really take your fancy at present.

24 FRIDAY

Moon Age Day 27 • Moon Sign Pisces

am . . . .

pm . . . .
Perhaps you have the right to seek a little peace and quiet, at least that is the way it seems to you today. Not everyone takes kindly to this frame of mind and there are times when you will simply have to explain yourself. All the same, real friends will be happy to give you the time you need to be alone.

25 SATURDAY

Moon Age Day 28 • Moon Sign Aries

am . . . .

pm . . . .
The Sun is now in your solar first house and ahead of the lunar high a period of real excitement and possibility opens up for you. This would be an ideal time to take any journey or for thinking through your personal strategy at work. More responsibility is likely in the not too distant future.

26 SUNDAY

Moon Age Day 0 • Moon Sign Aries

am . . . .

pm . . . .
Before today is out the Moon returns to your sign, consolidating the favourable trends that stand around you in any case and allowing you all the energy you need to realise that you are making excellent headway. Make time for love, which shines down on you in abundance today and tomorrow.

← NEGATIVE TREND						POSITIVE TREND →				
-5	-4	-3	-2	-1	LOVE	+1	+2	+3	+4	+5
					MONEY					
					LUCK					
					VITALITY					

27 MONDAY
Moon Age Day 1 • Moon Sign Taurus

am ....

pm ....
You are still in the right frame of mind to get what you want from life. Almost everyone that you come across has pretty much the same idea and the world should really be your oyster for the moment. Keeping up a pretence is a waste of time so abandon the idea when it seems opportune to do so.

28 TUESDAY
Moon Age Day 2 • Moon Sign Taurus

am ....

pm ....
With Tuesday might come a time when you can at least sit back and take stock of situations. Now you probably feel the need to spend some time in the company of family members and will want to listen to what they have to say. Chances are that you will be surprised!

29 WEDNESDAY
Moon Age Day 3 • Moon Sign Gemini

am ....

pm ....
A day when you keep yourself very busy, even if there is not really all that much to get done. The support that comes from the people you really love is very welcome, though in the main you know best what direction your life should be taking. Speed is not important, but accuracy is.

30 THURSDAY
Moon Age Day 4 • Moon Sign Gemini

am ....

pm ....
You can handle several different jobs at the same time today and will be forcing your opinions forward, even on those occasions when they have not been sought. A fairly stubborn Taurean is on the cards on this Thursday and few people would willingly tell you that your opinions are wrong.

1 FRIDAY

Moon Age Day 5 • Moon Sign Cancer

am ....

pm ....
The first day of May brings tasks and responsibilities that you may think
you have been ignoring recently. The truth is that you have simply been
weighing things up in your mind, or at least that is what you can tell
others. Once you get into gear today all sorts of things get done.

2 SATURDAY

Moon Age Day 6 • Moon Sign Cancer

am ....

pm ....
Activities in the outside world could seem to be a little uneventful, but
this is an illusion brought about because you are in a slightly lethargic
frame of mind. You can't keep going at full speed all the time and simply
have to take a rest now and again. Anxiety can be pushed aside for a
while.

3 SUNDAY

Moon Age Day 7 • Moon Sign Leo

am ....

pm ....
Some of your romantic fantasies stand a chance of coming good at
present, or at least they do if you put yourself in the right position to gain
from them. Space to think through a new business plan is not all that
easy to find, though all Taureans show a practical face to the world very
soon.

← *NEGATIVE TREND*								*POSITIVE TREND* →			
-5	-4	-3	-2	-1			+1	+2	+3	+4	+5
					LOVE						
					MONEY						
					LUCK						
					VITALITY						

1998

YOUR MONTH AT A GLANCE

The twelve numbered boxes represent the important areas in your life. The key to the numbers you will find beneath the panel. A sun above the number indicates that opportunities are around. A cloud below the number, that you should be a bit defensive. Nothing above or below and life will be pretty ordinary.

1	2	3	4	5	6	7	8	9	10	11	12

KEY

1 Strength of Personality
2 Personal Finance
3 Useful Information Gathering
4 Domestic Affairs
5 Pleasure & Romance
6 Effective Work & Health

7 One to One Relationships
8 Questioning, Thinking & Deciding
9 External Influences / Education
10 Career Aspirations
11 Teamwork Activities
12 Unconscious Impulses

MAY HIGHS AND LOWS

Here, I show how the rhythm of the Moon will affect you this month. Like the tide, your energies and abilities will rise and fall with its pattern. When it is above the date line, go-for-it. When it is below the line you should be resting.

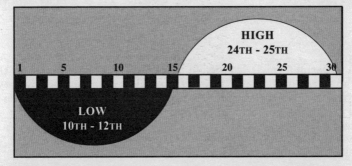

4 MONDAY

Moon Age Day 8 • Moon Sign Leo

am...

pm...
You will be happy to put yourself at the front of any new venture that you have helped to plan. Looking ahead, you may also see the sense in certain travel arrangements that could have an association with business as well as with pleasure. Leave controversy alone if you get the chance.

5 TUESDAY

Moon Age Day 9 • Moon Sign Virgo

am...

pm...
Whilst you clearly have much confidence at your disposal today, it is doubtful whether you will actually find anything much to do with it. This could prove to be a little frustrating, but you can always turn situations round if you wish. But is it really worth the effort swimming against the tide?

6 WEDNESDAY

Moon Age Day 10 • Moon Sign Virgo

am...

pm...
Your powers of attraction are particularly good today, which is why you may be concentrating your mind in the direction of love. An excellent period for popping any important question or for coming to terms with a definite change of attitude on the part of someone who is very important to you.

7 THURSDAY

Moon Age Day 11 • Moon Sign Virgo

am...

pm...
On a material level, today should prove to be quite productive. If there are any problems at all they will probably be associated with your personal life, which might not be running quite as smoothly. You will need a careful tongue and a great deal of tact when dealing with awkward types now.

8 FRIDAY
Moon Age Day 12 • Moon Sign Libra

am ....

pm ....
Certain loved ones could still be causing you the odd problem and though
these are not likely to last for any any length of time you will probably
be happy enough to spend some hours with friends. They are least
should be on your wavelength and willing to listen to your point of view.

9 SATURDAY
Moon Age Day 13 • Moon Sign Libra

am ....

pm ....
The leadership qualities which are often muted in the case of Taurus are
now showing much more clearly. This means that this stage of the week
should prove to be quite exciting and offer you the scope to spread your
wings. Meanwhile, personal matters should also be improving somewhat.

10 SUNDAY
Moon Age Day 14 • Moon Sign Scorpio

am ....

pm ....
Things are more or less certain to be slow for a day or two, thanks to the
present position of the Moon. You can use today to consolidate any gains
that you made earlier on and for dreaming up new schemes that will
apply later. Once again friends should be rallying to help you out if they
can.

← *NEGATIVE TREND*						*POSITIVE TREND*	→			
-5	-4	-3	-2	-1			+1	+2	+3	+4	+5
					LOVE						
					MONEY						
					LUCK						
					VITALITY						

11 MONDAY

Moon Age Day 15 • Moon Sign Scorpio

am ....

pm ....
A good day for catching up on any reading you might have to do and for taking some hours to think about domestic matters. It's unlikely that you would want to burn the candle at both ends right now and it would be just as well to make certain that you get some rest ahead of a busy spell.

12 TUESDAY

Moon Age Day 16 • Moon Sign Scorpio

am ....

pm ....
You really do need to do things your own way today and that could mean rubbing someone else up the wrong way unless you are especially careful. There should be more energy to call on and you are likely to be anxious to get on with jobs that those around you seem determined to delay.

13 WEDNESDAY

Moon Age Day 17 • Moon Sign Sagittarius

am ....

pm ....
The greatest gains to be made at the moment come as a result of your ability to bring others round to your way of thinking. All in all this should not be difficult today and you have all the charm and kindness at your disposal that you could possibly need. You show great confidence in yourself.

14 THURSDAY

Moon Age Day 18 • Moon Sign Sagittarius

am ....

pm ....
Someone at work, or a loved one, if your work is at home, could prove especially difficult to deal with today and if this turns out to be the case it might be better not to try. Creating space to allow your plans to mature is also uppermost in your mind and you have some sparkling ideas later.

15 FRIDAY
Moon Age Day 19 • Moon Sign Capricorn

am...

pm...
You are certainly not much of a home bird today and would be more than willing to spread your wings on any occasion that it proves possible for you to do so. Many of your potential successes at the moment come down to a particular frame of mind and depend upon belief in yourself.

16 SATURDAY
Moon Age Day 20 • Moon Sign Capricorn

am...

pm...
With Mercury in your solar first house others should find you particularly interesting to be around at present. The power of your communication is especially well marked and you should be able to bring almost anyone round to a point of view that is distinctly reasonable and sound.

17 SUNDAY
Moon Age Day 21 • Moon Sign Capricorn

am...

pm...
Things come together in a positive way, so that you should be fairly happy with what you manage to achieve today. Reasoning things out is not at all difficult, even though there are some people who seem determined to be awkward. These types you simply manage to take in your stride.

← *NEGATIVE TREND*						*POSITIVE TREND* →				
-5	-4	-3	-2	-1		+1	+2	+3	+4	+5
					LOVE					
					MONEY					
					LUCK					
					VITALITY					

18 MONDAY
Moon Age Day 22 • Moon Sign Aquarius

am ....

pm ....
You are as open and generous today as your sign of Taurus can be.
Creative and inspiring you manage to instil your own present optimism
into just about everyone you come across. Comfort and security take
something of a back seat in favour of a more dynamic mode of thinking.

19 TUESDAY
Moon Age Day 23 • Moon Sign Aquarius

am ....

pm ....
Keeping up a high social profile you now manage to convert the awkward
types who were causing you slight problems earlier in the week. Part of
the reason for this is that you have more time at your disposal and will
be able to use reasoned thinking in your dealings with the world at large.

20 WEDNESDAY
Moon Age Day 24 • Moon Sign Pisces

am ....

pm ....
It is true that you feel the need to make your opinions known today. This
is all well and good but unless you include tact in the recipe you could
come slightly unstuck. In the main the day should be a good one
however, and much depends on the support you gain from those around
you.

21 THURSDAY
Moon Age Day 25 • Moon Sign Pisces

am ....

pm ....
A more stable trend relating to money comes along, thanks to the
changing position of the Sun in your chart. It is possible that you may
now be able to plan ahead more successfully and that you will be able to
take the odd chance with finances. Routines may get on your nerves a
little.

22 FRIDAY
Moon Age Day 26 • Moon Sign Aries

am ....

pm ....
The present position of Mars in your chart stimulates a more competitive phase that is having a bearing on your life for the next few weeks. The more practical qualities of Taurus now begin to shine out and it is really amazing just how much you manage to get done during this phase.

23 SATURDAY
Moon Age Day 27 • Moon Sign Aries

am ....

pm ....
A brief period when you are best served by keeping yourself to yourself.. Secrets probably mean a great deal to you at the moment and you are anxious to keep tight lipped about a particular plan that is of importance to you. At least hours spent alone mean time to genuinely rest.

24 SUNDAY
Moon Age Day 28 • Moon Sign Taurus

am ....

pm ....
The Moon, returning to your sign, now brings a more stimulating and interesting period than you might have experienced at any stage during this month. With confidence going out through the roof this is definitely a time to be doing whatever takes your personal fancy.

← NEGATIVE TREND								POSITIVE TREND →			
-5	-4	-3	-2	-1			+1	+2	+3	+4	+5
					LOVE						
					MONEY						
					LUCK						
					VITALITY						

25 MONDAY   *Moon Age Day 0 • Moon Sign Taurus*

am ....

pm ....
A good time for fresh starts of any sort and for making improvements to
your life on just about any level. The icing on the cake is the treatment
you receive from others, since it is obvious that they really do have your
best interests at heart in the days that lie ahead.

26 TUESDAY   *Moon Age Day 1 • Moon Sign Gemini*

am ....

pm ....
A good day for making financial decisions, though probably not so
positive a period as yesterday. If this period offers you the first real
chance of the Spring to get out and about, you would do well to do so. Not
everyone at home is especially easy to deal with at present.

27 WEDNESDAY   *Moon Age Day 2 • Moon Sign Gemini*

am ....

pm ....
The business of the day tends to be plain sailing but might not be quite
as exciting as you wish. If this turns out to be the case you can either wait
until things improve of their own accord, or else make a determined
effort to speed any particular process up for yourself. A positive attitude
counts.

28 THURSDAY   *Moon Age Day 3 • Moon Sign Cancer*

am ....

pm ....
Adaptability is the word for today, and this isn't always a commodity that
Taurus finds easy to muster. The more flexible you stay in your opinions
and attitudes, the better things should be for you generally. Creating a
good impression socially is not difficult however and presents the best
opportunities.

29 FRIDAY
Moon Age Day 4 • Moon Sign Cancer

am . . . .

pm . . . .
The business of the day is easy to deal with and relationships look especially good too. Today marks an important interlude when you would be more than willing to make the most of any new chance to advance yourself that comes your way. Don't be frightened at any stage to say 'Yes'.

30 SATURDAY
Moon Age Day 5 • Moon Sign Cancer

am . . . .

pm . . . .
A brand new boost to love life and personal relationships generally comes along as Venus moves into your solar first house. The planet is going to be there for a while and even existing relationships look stronger and more meaningful with this positive planetary position coming along.

31 SUNDAY
Moon Age Day 6 • Moon Sign Leo

am . . . .

pm . . . .
A pleasant day for simply pleasing yourself, and the more so if you manage to be away from work and out at the coast or in the country. A time to allow dreams to flow and mix, giving you the chance to use them to your advantage later on. Confidence is not lacking, but not really necessary either.

← *NEGATIVE TREND*								*POSITIVE TREND* →		
-5	-4	-3	-2	-1			+1	+2	+3	+4	+5
					LOVE						
					MONEY						
					LUCK						
					VITALITY						

1998

YOUR MONTH AT A GLANCE

The twelve numbered boxes represent the important areas in your life. The key to the numbers you will find beneath the panel. A sun above the number indicates that opportunities are around. A cloud below the number, that you should be a bit defensive. Nothing above or below and life will be pretty ordinary.

1	2	3	4	5	6	7	8	9	10	11	12

KEY

1 Strength of Personality
2 Personal Finance
3 Useful Information Gathering
4 Domestic Affairs
5 Pleasure & Romance
6 Effective Work & Health

7 One to One Relationships
8 Questioning, Thinking & Deciding
9 External Influences / Education
10 Career Aspirations
11 Teamwork Activities
12 Unconscious Impulses

JUNE HIGHS AND LOWS

Here, I show how the rhythm of the Moon will affect you this month. Like the tide, your energies and abilities will rise and fall with its pattern. When it is above the date line, go-for-it. When it is below the line you should be resting.

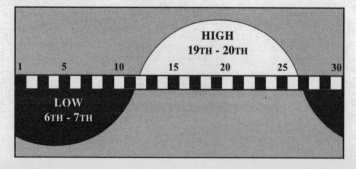

1 MONDAY
Moon Age Day 7 • Moon Sign Leo

am ....

pm ....
There is a strong emphasis on finances at present and you may want to get one or two money matters sorted out before the day is very old. An early holiday at this time would certainly benefit Taureans, but if you can't get away do try to get at least a few hours to yourself at some stage.

2 TUESDAY
Moon Age Day 8 • Moon Sign Virgo

am ....

pm ....
Positive highlights surround romance, which is working the way you would wish it to at present. This is the area of life where you should concentrate your efforts. If you are single, this might be as good a time as any to form a new relationship, or to tell someone how you really feel.

3 WEDNESDAY
Moon Age Day 9 • Moon Sign Virgo

am ....

pm ....
A boost to your fortunes should come along in the form of a more inspiring phase emotionally and with regard to matters of love. Today is a time when you should catch up on rest, though this may be of a positive kind and could involve some fairly hectic activity paradoxically.

4 THURSDAY
Moon Age Day 10 • Moon Sign Libra

am ....

pm ....
The trends today stimulate your typical Taurean qualities so that you should not find it too difficult to get along with the people you come into contact with. With a combination of patience and perseverance it's fairly easy to get what you want from life during a positive spell.

5 FRIDAY
Moon Age Day 11 • Moon Sign Libra

am...

pm...
Work and practical issues could seem to be a bit of a grind at the start
of today, so that it might take you a little while to get fully into gear. If
energy is slightly lacking it might be a good idea to find something
different to do. At least that way you'll be ringing the changes.

6 SATURDAY
Moon Age Day 12 • Moon Sign Scorpio

am...

pm...
If things were not exactly sparkling yesterday it was because you were
registering the commencement of the lunar low. Of course it still has a
bearing on your life today, but the truth is that opportunity can still
knock, so don't turn yourself into a hermit. Stay out in the mainstream.

7 SUNDAY
Moon Age Day 13 • Moon Sign Scorpio

am...

pm...
Push on through the slightly less favourable patch and continue to keep
faith with your own good ideas. Before today is out you may discover that
you have been making progress all along. Friends and relatives alike
seem to be putting themselves out to please you right now.

	← *NEGATIVE TREND*								*POSITIVE TREND* →			
-5	-4	-3	-2	-1				+1	+2	+3	+4	+5
					LOVE							
					MONEY							
					LUCK							
					VITALITY							

8 MONDAY   *Moon Age Day 14 • Moon Sign Sagittarius*

am ....

pm ....
All of a sudden it seems as though everyone wants to be in your good books, and it's all thanks to a combination of simply being the way you are and the position of Venus in your solar chart. Your popularity is certainly not in doubt and neither is your ability to score significant successes.

9 TUESDAY   *Moon Age Day 15 • Moon Sign Sagittarius*

am ....

pm ....
Though some of your best intentions might be misconstrued by others that is no reason to abandon them. If you carry on as you see fit, those around you will soon see the sense in what you are saying. However, you can't bulldoze schemes through, no matter how much you would wish to.

10 WEDNESDAY   *Moon Age Day 16 • Moon Sign Sagittarius*

am ....

pm ....
If you have one or two ingenious ideas as to how to increase your bank balance, it might be a good idea, before you get cracking, to have a word with someone in the know. Get rich quick schemes probably will not be working all that well for you right now and slow and steady usually wins better.

11 THURSDAY   *Moon Age Day 17 • Moon Sign Capricorn*

am ....

pm ....
You need a break from mundane responsibilities so that you can expand your personal horizons a little during the main part of this working week. It might seem a bit of a paradox to slow down in order to get more done, but as far as you are concerned it should work well.

12 FRIDAY
Moon Age Day 18 • Moon Sign Capricorn

am ....

pm ....
Much of what you value in life at the moment is more or less certain to
be seen in material terms. It isn't that you are in the least selfish, or that
you want to possess a great deal. The truth is that you are simply facing
a few honest to goodness facts and there is nothing wrong with that.

13 SATURDAY
Moon Age Day 19 • Moon Sign Aquarius

am ....

pm ....
You show a great tendency to get ahead at the moment, though you
should have at least one eye over your shoulder since there are a few
people about who could think that you are ignoring them. Of course this
isn't really true - is it? Your personality shines out today.

14 SUNDAY
Moon Age Day 20 • Moon Sign Aquarius

am ....

pm ....
Looking and feeling at your best there is little doubt that you are causing
a few heads to turn as you go along your merry way right now. Take
advantage of the situation because there is help on offer that would
normally surprise you. Financially speaking there might be a good
phase coming.

← NEGATIVE TREND							POSITIVE TREND →			
-5	-4	-3	-2	-1		+1	+2	+3	+4	+5
					LOVE					
					MONEY					
					LUCK					
					VITALITY					

15 MONDAY *Moon Age Day 21 • Moon Sign Pisces*

am . . . .

pm . . . .
The pace of your everyday life quickens significantly, leaving you with little enough time to monitor everything that is going on around you. If life turns out to be something of a blur, you can at least be sure that there are people watching out for your best interests. Popularity is high.

16 TUESDAY *Moon Age Day 22 • Moon Sign Pisces*

am . . . .

pm . . . .
Although a specific friend may seem to let you down today, the truth is that you could easily have laid yourself open to the situation. Someone you have not seen for quite a while could easily be playing a much more important role in your life at present and there are many facts to balance.

17 WEDNESDAY *Moon Age Day 23 • Moon Sign Aries*

am . . . .

pm . . . .
Although it is fairly unusual for your sign you tend to show just the smallest trace of arrogance in your dealings with others at present. Be careful, because there could be a few chickens coming home to roost eventually as a result of your behaviour today. Tolerance is necessary.

18 THURSDAY *Moon Age Day 24 • Moon Sign Aries*

am . . . .

pm . . . .
A period begins during which you can pick up some very important information. Today is not about talking so much as listening, and since everyone else seems to be making so much noise, it shouldn't prove to be all that difficult to find the sort of material that you can turn to your own advantage.

19 FRIDAY

Moon Age Day 25 • Moon Sign Taurus

am ....

pm ....

Outside pressures and the general pace of life conspire to restrict your efforts a little on this Tuesday. That is no reason for relaxing your efforts however, because if you were ever in the right mood to succeed against all the odds, you certainly are now. Confidence is certainly not lacking.

20 SATURDAY

Moon Age Day 26 • Moon Sign Taurus

am ....

pm ....

The result of all your efforts yesterday becomes obvious now that the Moon has taken up residence in your own sign again. This is a go-getting period, thanks to the effort that you have already put in. Creating the right sort of atmosphere for personal advancement should be a piece of cake.

21 SUNDAY

Moon Age Day 27 • Moon Sign Gemini

am ....

pm ....

The Sun comes into your solar third house and means a month long period when you will be doing all that you can to get your message across to other people. Powers of communication are really good and you should also find that you have a particular affinity with Gemini born individuals.

← *NEGATIVE TREND*							*POSITIVE TREND* →			
-5	-4	-3	-2	-1	LOVE		+1	+2	+3	+4	+5
					MONEY						
					LUCK						
					VITALITY						

122

22 MONDAY   *Moon Age Day 28 • Moon Sign Gemini*

am ....

pm ....
Avoid being too possessive, especially in a relationship sense. Whatever
the issue, you can have what you want better if you are willing to give
it away first. There is a certain Taurean tendency to cling too tightly,
which is is clearly something that you would want to avoid at this stage.

23 TUESDAY   *Moon Age Day 29 • Moon Sign Cancer*

am ....

pm ....
Short-term plans have to be shelved today, probably in favour of no real
plan at all. This mode of thinking suits certain other signs of the zodiac
better than it does yours, though it is possible for you to detach yourself
if you really try. Life knows best for you today, and you have to realise
the fact.

24 WEDNESDAY   *Moon Age Day 0 • Moon Sign Cancer*

am ....

pm ....
Attracting money and the more pleasurable associations of life couldn't
be easier. You really are coming into your own now and should find
yourself to be entering a phase that is both pleasurable and entertaining.
The end Wednesday is likely to bring a surprise or two, especially
personally.

25 THURSDAY   *Moon Age Day 1 • Moon Sign Cancer*

am ....

pm ....
One main task is your best way to achievement, and is a technique that
is comfortable for you. Certain matters have to be put to one side today,
in favour of chasing a particular objective. What is more, you have the
ability to enlist just about all the support you could possibly need on the
way.

26 FRIDAY

Moon Age Day 2 • Moon Sign Leo

am. . . . .

pm. . . . .
Whilst much effort is being put into your life at the present time, don't forget that your third house Sun is now offering you tremendous incentives in terms of speaking out. You could probably save yourself a great deal of effort simply by asking for what you want. Hey presto, you get it.

27 SATURDAY

Moon Age Day 3 • Moon Sign Leo

am. . . . .

pm. . . . .
A minor professional setback is on the way, but take note of the word 'minor'. Once you have had time to think things through, you can get through, over or round any potential problem. Once again those better powers of communication are also likely to come to your aid when you are most needy.

28 SUNDAY

Moon Age Day 4 • Moon Sign Virgo

am. . . . .

pm. . . . .
Discussions relating to romantic issues take on a new urgency and a new importance today. You have a charming personality when you take the time to turn it up to full power and there is little doubt that you can get your own way if you really want to. But is that what you want right now?

← NEGATIVE TREND						POSITIVE TREND →				
-5	-4	-3	-2	-1		+1	+2	+3	+4	+5
LOVE										
MONEY										
LUCK										
VITALITY										

29 MONDAY
Moon Age Day 5 • Moon Sign Virgo

am ....

pm ....
Keep your eyes and ears open because it is truly surprising what waits around every corner at the moment. Gains come from the most unlikely directions and it would be good to offer yourself an advantage by being in the right place at the most opportune time. Love plays an important role.

30 TUESDAY
Moon Age Day 6 • Moon Sign Virgo

am ....

pm ....
Your home environment becomes more comfortable, or at least that may be how it appears to be for the moment. The truth is that you are probably taking the opportunity to sit back and take stock of all you have to be grateful for. An easier path personally seems to be yours for the taking.

1 WENESDAY
Moon Age Day 7 • Moon Sign Libra

am ....

pm ....
A day of rather pressing obligations appears to be your lot. Of course you could easily walk away from most of them and it is true to say that they will still be around tomorrow. Confidences are coming your way and it really suits your own needs to treat them as such in the days ahead.

2 THURSDAY
Moon Age Day 8 • Moon Sign Libra

am ....

pm ....
Keep up the pressure and make certain that you are having a good time generally. There is no point in allowing little things to get you down, especially when there is so much going for you in a general sense. Attitude is all important, particularly when dealing with family members.

3 FRIDAY

Moon Age Day 9 • Moon Sign Libra

am . . . .

pm . . . .
The potential for success still looks fairly good, though your powers of
communication might not be all that you would wish for just at present.
It won't be long before you find you have the potential to talk the hind
leg of a donkey, though a quiet interlude may well suit you in any case.

4 SATURDAY

Moon Age Day 10 • Moon Sign Scorpio

am . . . .

pm . . . .
The weekend brings its own form of rewards, even if these tend to be of
a fairly low key sort. It's true that you should have the potential to get
out and about, and you can make the most of slight changes to
circumstances at home. Keep an open mind about potential changes to
finances.

5 SUNDAY

Moon Age Day 11 • Moon Sign Scorpio

am . . . .

pm . . . .
You revel now in the company of some fairly unusual sorts of people.
Rewards are yours for the taking, that is if you recognise the sort of
potential that rests within you. A good day for planning the week ahead,
though leaving just a little time to rest yourself ahead of the new week.

← NEGATIVE TREND							POSITIVE TREND →				
-5	-4	-3	-2	-1			+1	+2	+3	+4	+5
					LOVE						
					MONEY						
					LUCK						
					VITALITY						

1998

YOUR MONTH AT A GLANCE

The twelve numbered boxes represent the important areas in your life. The key to the numbers you will find beneath the panel. A sun above the number indicates that opportunities are around. A cloud below the number, that you should be a bit defensive. Nothing above or below and life will be pretty ordinary.

1	2	3	4	5	6	7	8	9	10	11	12

KEY

1 Strength of Personality
2 Personal Finance
3 Useful Information Gathering
4 Domestic Affairs
5 Pleasure & Romance
6 Effective Work & Health

7 One to One Relationships
8 Questioning, Thinking & Deciding
9 External Influences / Education
10 Career Aspirations
11 Teamwork Activities
12 Unconscious Impulses

JULY HIGHS AND LOWS

Here, I show how the rhythm of the Moon will affect you this month. Like the tide, your energies and abilities will rise and fall with its pattern. When it is above the date line, go-for-it. When it is below the line you should be resting.

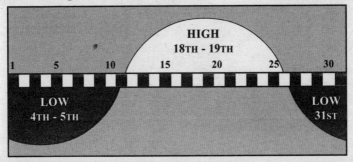

6 MONDAY
Moon Age Day 12 • Moon Sign Sagittarius

am ....

pm ....
Mars is entering your solar third house, so you won't be at all backward when it comes to saying what you think for the next few days. This is not at all a bad thing, but you might find that you can upset one or two people without really intending to do so. Tact is still very important.

7 TUESDAY
Moon Age Day 13 • Moon Sign Sagittarius

am ....

pm ....
You seem to be rather too ready to accept the views of other people at present, which is all well and good if you really are certain that their opinions are sensible. Rewards tend to come thick and fast at work, and it is important that you come to recognise them as such during this week.

8 WEDNESDAY
Moon Age Day 14 • Moon Sign Sagittarius

am ....

pm ....
A rather sudden and unexpected series of events could mark today out as being rather special. There is plenty to keep you occupied and you won't go short of the right sort of company either. Not a time to rest on your laurels when it comes to speaking out, and you have great determination now.

9 THURSDAY
Moon Age Day 15 • Moon Sign Capricorn

am ....

pm ....
Important decisions made today are likely to serve you well for a considerable time to come. You should not underestimate your own ability to make a favourable impression and it is the right time to tell others what you really think. Perhaps the most important day of the month, all things considered.

10 FRIDAY
Moon Age Day 16 • Moon Sign Capricorn

am ....

pm ....
You are likely to find others agreeing with what you have to say, partly because they would not dare do otherwise. Check your motives very carefully at present and make certain that you are not railroading friends and relatives into situations that are not at all of their own choosing.

11 SATURDAY
Moon Age Day 17 • Moon Sign Aquarius

am ....

pm ....
There is a slight self-defeating tendency about you this Saturday. Perhaps you do not think yourself equal to some task that you are expected to take on. If this is the case either modify the job so that it suits you better, or leave it alone altogether. Some practical help is on offer now.

12 SUNDAY
Moon Age Day 18 • Moon Sign Aquarius

am ....

pm ....
Domestic situations are likely to be particularly important, which is probably not all that surprising on a Sunday. The fact that it is the weekend should mean that you have a little more time to devote to the people who are important in your life from a personal point of view.

← NEGATIVE TREND						POSITIVE TREND →				
-5	-4	-3	-2	-1		+1	+2	+3	+4	+5
					LOVE					
					MONEY					
					LUCK					
					VITALITY					

13 MONDAY
Moon Age Day 19 • Moon Sign Pisces

am...

pm...
Friendship is very important to you at the present time, more especially because there are also practical gains to be made from looking after those you care for. You won't abandon someone who is in trouble and your loyalty does not go without a reward in the fullness of time.

14 TUESDAY
Moon Age Day 20 • Moon Sign Pisces

am...

pm...
Don't leave travel arrangements until the last minute. The truth is that you may really want to spread your wings this year and it is possible that you have something in mind that is really exciting. Take other people into your confidence now, even if distant travel is not a possibility.

15 WEDNESDAY
Moon Age Day 21 • Moon Sign Aries

am...

pm...
Don't complicate life by getting yourself into a dull mood or by thinking about situations that you can do nothing to alter. It would be far better to cast your mind forward to the future and to decide what you want to do in conjunction with your nearest and dearest.

16 THURSDAY
Moon Age Day 22 • Moon Sign Aries

am...

pm...
Another fairly decisive period comes along now, ahead of your lunar high. Get your mind in gear today and don't allow irrelevant details to hold you back if you have any choice in the matter. An atmospheric time emotionally and a period when love is likely to come knocking at your door.

17 FRIDAY
Moon Age Day 23 • Moon Sign Aries

am ....

pm ....
The lunar high ushers in a time of great conviction for you, which means you have a great deal of power to change circumstances that have not really suited you in the past. Creating the right space to please yourself will not be difficult and you do your best to be of use to others as well.

18 SATURDAY
Moon Age Day 24 • Moon Sign Taurus

am ....

pm ....
Things are still looking fairly good for you and with everything to play for you will not mind being out there at the forefront of life. Not everyone appears to have your best interests at heart and it is just possible that they may have a rational and sensible point of view.

19 SUNDAY
Moon Age Day 25 • Moon Sign Taurus

am ....

pm ....
You are able to bring out the very best in others now that things have slowed down a little and you have some time to stop and think properly. With a quieter schedule in the offing, you might deliberately choose to spend and hour or two in the company of family members or really good friends.

← *NEGATIVE TREND*							*POSITIVE TREND* →			
-5	-4	-3	-2	-1		+1	+2	+3	+4	+5
					LOVE					
					MONEY					
					LUCK					
					VITALITY					

20 MONDAY
Moon Age Day 26 • Moon Sign Gemini

am ....

pm ....

As you start a new working week don't be surprised if a great deal of what you have to do has already been planned. This could mean a week of tying up loose ends, which could turn out to be a little tedious if you are not careful. Space to be yourself is the gift that is on offer - so take it.

21 TUESDAY
Moon Age Day 27 • Moon Sign Gemini

am ....

pm ....

A little positive thinking could go a long way at this stage of the week and month. The more you can convince yourself that you know what you are doing, the better things are going to turn out for you in a general sense. This is not a time to stay safely in the shadows, no matter how you feel.

22 WEDNESDAY
Moon Age Day 28 • Moon Sign Cancer

am ....

pm ....

Dwelling on matters from the past, about which you can do nothing, is certainly not the way to proceed on this day. Routines of any sort are likely to get you down and there is a great need to please yourself and to find new interests wherever possible. You need plenty of variety.

23 THURSDAY
Moon Age Day 0 • Moon Sign Cancer

am ....

pm ....

With the Sun now entering your solar fourth house you are in a month long period when family matters become more important to you than has been the case in the recent past. You should find plenty of time to consider the opinions of family members and to discuss matters with them.

24 FRIDAY
Moon Age Day 1 • Moon Sign Leo

am..

pm..
You may be a little less than forthcoming in social situations, though this is probably because you are not really in a position to mix with the sort of people who are most important to you in a specific sense. All the same there are some fairly influential types about and they could be useful.

25 SATURDAY
Moon Age Day 2 • Moon Sign Leo

am..

pm..
Others will not expect you to be quite as assertive as you turn out to be today, so you might be taking a few people by surprise. This is probably no bad thing since you are in a position to catch them off guard and to get what you want from them before they realise what is happening.

26 SUNDAY
Moon Age Day 3 • Moon Sign Virgo

am..

pm..
Leisure and pleasure matters mean a great deal to you today, which is probably understandable on a Sunday. In a personal sense there is everything to play for and you revel in the company of your partner or a loved one. A good day for getting out to the coast or the country.

← *NEGATIVE TREND*						*POSITIVE TREND* →				
-5	-4	-3	-2	-1		+1	+2	+3	+4	+5
					LOVE					
					MONEY					
					LUCK					
					VITALITY					

27 MONDAY
Moon Age Day 4 • Moon Sign Virgo

am..

pm..
You may be caught between trying to please those around you and doing what seems to be right for you personally. You cannot expect to make any sort of gain if you are not being truthful to your self. In the end your own choices count, and will suit the people you care about as well.

28 TUESDAY
Moon Age Day 5 • Moon Sign Virgo

am..

pm..
Lighthearted conversations really do suit you the best today and you will not really want to explore the deeper recesses of your own life, or that of others. Keep your touch gentle and patient and you cannot go far wrong. A much more successful day than you would possibly expect at its start.

29 WEDNESDAY
Moon Age Day 6 • Moon Sign Libra

am..

pm..
Positive changes look possible and the planning of them could take up a great deal of your time right now. People of all types are likely to cross your path and will have plenty to offer you in the way of advice. How much of it you will take notice of seems to be in some doubt however.

30 THURSDAY
Moon Age Day 7 • Moon Sign Libra

am..

pm..
Get as much from work as you possibly can, because it would be fair to say that your personal life may leave just a little to be desired for today. It is the attitude of those closest to you which is rather difficult to understand and you can only really wait and see what transpires in the fullness of time.

31 FRIDAY ♦ *Moon Age Day 8 • Moon Sign Scorpio*

am . . . .

pm . . . .
The lunar low sees you finishing the month on a rather quiet note. Not that this is necessarily a bad thing because it is clear that you have been burning the candle at both ends for quite a while now. End the working week quietly and efficiently and prepare for a happy weekend.

1 SATURDAY ♦ *Moon Age Day 9 • Moon Sign Scorpio*

am . . . .

pm . . . .
A happy weekend was in prospect and that is what most of you will find, though you cannot expect to be firing on all cylinders and will be happiest taking a little time out to do whatever takes your fancy. Keep away from tedious types because you are not especially patient today.

2 SUNDAY ♦ *Moon Age Day 10 • Moon Sign Sagittarius*

am . . . .

pm . . . .
The lunar low leaves you behind and allows a slightly more exciting sort of day than you probably managed yesterday. If any sort of travel is in prospect you need to be doing some careful planning now. This may also be a good day for family discussions of some sort.

← *NEGATIVE TREND*								*POSITIVE TREND* →			
-5	-4	-3	-2	-1			+1	+2	+3	+4	+5
					LOVE						
					MONEY						
					LUCK						
					VITALITY						

1998

YOUR MONTH AT A GLANCE

The twelve numbered boxes represent the important areas in your life. The key to the numbers you will find beneath the panel. A sun above the number indicates that opportunities are around. A cloud below the number, that you should be a bit defensive. Nothing above or below and life will be pretty ordinary.

| 1 | 2 | 3 | 4 | 5 | 6 | 7 | 8 | 9 | 10 | 11 | 12 |

KEY

1 Strength of Personality
2 Personal Finance
3 Useful Information Gathering
4 Domestic Affairs
5 Pleasure & Romance
6 Effective Work & Health

7 One to One Relationships
8 Questioning, Thinking & Deciding
9 External Influences / Education
10 Career Aspirations
11 Teamwork Activities
12 Unconscious Impulses

AUGUST HIGHS AND LOWS

Here, I show how the rhythm of the Moon will affect you this month. Like the tide, your energies and abilities will rise and fall with its pattern. When it is above the date line, go-for-it. When it is below the line you should be resting.

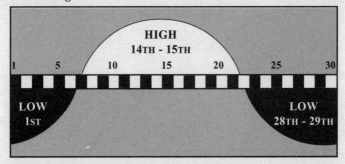

HIGH
14TH - 15TH

1   5   10   15   20   25   30

LOW
1ST

LOW
28TH - 29TH

3 MONDAY ♦ *Moon Age Day 11 • Moon Sign Sagittarius*

am ....

pm ....
You should be more than determined to have your own way today, which is no bad thing just as long as you bear the needs of others in mind too. Keep up the pressure to move in the direction that you want in a career sense and stay as true as you can to your personal ideals.

4 TUESDAY ♦ *Moon Age Day 12 • Moon Sign Sagittarius*

am ....

pm ....
Some happy news is likely to be coming your way at some stage today. It could be that family members have something good to tell you, or the fact that a friend has decided that your opinions are worth following. Either way, make it plain that you are happy with the outcome.

5 WEDNESDAY ♦ *Moon Age Day 13 • Moon Sign Capricorn*

am ....

pm ....
Variety certainly seems to be the spice of life as far as you are concerned today. So much is this the case that it might be a little difficult to know what you should concentrate on next. There are no end of unique and interesting possibilities about, some of which are personally intriguing.

6 THURSDAY ♦ *Moon Age Day 14 • Moon Sign Capricorn*

am ....

pm ....
The domestic routines that are a part of your life should be a cause of significant joy today, not least of all because your nearest and dearest are proving to be so very helpful. Not a good time for taking anyone for granted however and you will need to show how much you appreciate others.

7 FRIDAY ◆ *Moon Age Day 15 • Moon Sign Aquarius*

am..

pm..
Professional developments could have been rather taxing this week and it is likely that you are looking forward to the weekend as a result. All the same, you might discover today that you have been able to feather your nest in a quite unexpected and probably a very positive way.

8 SATURDAY ◆ *Moon Age Day 16 • Moon Sign Aquarius*

am..

pm..
The business of the day, and especially getting from A to B, could prove to be somewhat awkward. Every cloud has a silver lining and if you are forced to pause on your travels, you might be struck by one or two really original ideas. Chances are that these are worth pursuing.

9 SUNDAY ◆ *Moon Age Day 17 • Moon Sign Aquarius*

am..

pm..
Probably a day for making certain that your partner, or other loved ones, are being looked after properly. It isn't that you fail to monitor this fact most of the time, but you have had an especially busy week and a little extra love and attention never goes amiss in any case.

← *NEGATIVE TREND*						*POSITIVE TREND* →				
-5	-4	-3	-2	-1		+1	+2	+3	+4	+5
					LOVE					
					MONEY					
					LUCK					
					VITALITY					

10 MONDAY ♦ *Moon Age Day 18 • Moon Sign Pisces*

am . . . .

pm . . . .
It is possible that you are feeling distinctly nostalgic at this time and
want to push your mind back into the past. As long as you do not allow
such feelings to take you over there is no harm in them at present. All
the same, there are some pretty good opportunities facing you in the here
and now.

11 TUESDAY ♦ *Moon Age Day 19 • Moon Sign Pisces*

am . . . .

pm . . . .
Others find you kind, charming and co-operative. Because this is the
case you do not exactly have to go out of your way to be liked at present
and may have been trying a little too hard of late. Personal successes call
for a modicum of single-minded determination just at the present time.

12 WEDNESDAY ♦ *Moon Age Day 20 • Moon Sign Aries*

am . . . .

pm . . . .
Personal and social obligations are no problem to you at present, in fact
it might be suggested that they comprise the most interesting facets of
your life right now. Not only are you happy to put yourself out for other
people but you are able to make significant personal gains along the way.

13 THURSDAY ♦ *Moon Age Day 21 • Moon Sign Aries*

am . . . .

pm . . . .
A quieter day than of late, probably due to the fact that you are keen to
think things over. This means a little self-imposed isolation and the need
to batten down the hatches when it comes to communication. Although
there is no problem here, you may have to explain yourself.

14 FRIDAY ◆ *Moon Age Day 22 • Moon Sign Taurus*

am ....

pm ....
You can really be yourself again today and the force of your wonderfully
warm personality is really shining out. With the Moon in attendance and
everything to play for, you should be looking forward to the weekend and
all that it may have on offer. The best time for limited speculation.

15 SATURDAY ◆ *Moon Age Day 23 • Moon Sign Taurus*

am ....

pm ....
Getting ahead in a professional sense may not be all that easy at the
weekend and you will probably have to use all that energy up in personal
and family projects. Whatever you do choose, chances are that you do it
to the best of your ability, and with plenty of potential success.

16 SUNDAY ◆ *Moon Age Day 24 • Moon Sign Gemini*

am ....

pm ....
A practical or financial matter is sorted out very early in the day, almost
certainly leaving you with the feeling of a job well done. Personal
confidence is still not as high as it should be however and you need to
cultivate a slightly greater sense of your own importance at present.

← *NEGATIVE TREND*							*POSITIVE TREND*	→		
-5	-4	-3	-2	-1			+1	+2	+3	+4	+5
					LOVE						
					MONEY						
					LUCK						
					VITALITY						

17 MONDAY ♦ *Moon Age Day 25 • Moon Sign Gemini*

am . . . .

pm . . . .
There are certain aspects of life that you could be taking rather more
seriously than you should today. Remember that one or two people could
simply be having a little joke at your expense. The way to beat such types
is to refuse to take the bait. Matters are sorted out later on.

18 TUESDAY ♦ *Moon Age Day 26 • Moon Sign Cancer*

am . . . .

pm . . . .
Avoid too many mundane obligations early in the day and settle instead
for as many changes in routine as you can organise or manage. Confidence is not as high as it might be, which is yet another reasons to ring
the changes and to prove what you are truly worth when not tied down.

19 WEDNESDAY ♦ *Moon Age Day 27 • Moon Sign Cancer*

am . . . .

pm . . . .
There should be plenty of high spirits about today and no lack of
opportunity for you to put them to very good use. Active, almost from the
very moment that you get out of bed, the world is likely to be your oyster.
An ideal time for catching up on almost forgotten social contacts.

20 THURSDAY ♦ *Moon Age Day 28 • Moon Sign Leo*

am . . . .

pm . . . .
Home based matters are a little stirred up by present planetary happen-
ings. Almost certainly this leads to a few home truths and it is possible
that one or two of them will go against the grain a little as far as you are
concerned. Worrying about matters from the past is not recommended.

21 FRIDAY ♦ *Moon Age Day 0 • Moon Sign Leo*

am...

pm...
On the whole you are still pretty much in the limelight, even if this fact is not all that evident early in the day. Any slight discomfort in your life at the moment is unlikely to last all that long and you should find that you are fairly pleased to get your head together with like-minded types.

22 SATURDAY ♦ *Moon Age Day 1 • Moon Sign Leo*

am...

pm...
The freedom to simply be yourself is well marked today and you are off to a flying start when it comes to getting what you want from life. A close friends is displaying something of an attitude problem and some of that special Taurean tact is called for when it comes to dealing with them.

23 SUNDAY ♦ *Moon Age Day 2 • Moon Sign Virgo*

am...

pm...
A boost to your personality is made possible and you find that this is an ideal time for getting to the front of any queue in life. You do so, not because you are impatient, but simply because others are so willing to move aside for you. Interesting encounters of a personal kind are likely.

← *NEGATIVE TREND*					*POSITIVE TREND* →				
-5	-4	-3	-2	-1	+1	+2	+3	+4	+5
					LOVE				
					MONEY				
					LUCK				
					VITALITY				

24 MONDAY   *Moon Age Day 3 • Moon Sign Virgo*

am ....

pm ....
The best time of the month to be around house and home, even if work
responsibilities make this a little difficult until later in the day. There
is plenty to play for in an emotional sense and the people you really care
about the most are more than willing to put themselves out on your
behalf.

25 TUESDAY   *Moon Age Day 4 • Moon Sign Libra*

am ....

pm ....
Compromises are necessary if you really want to get the most out of life
today. Not all of them are easy to accommodate because it is a process
of negotiation. However, the really important areas do not see you losing
out and you should be able to get your message across easily.

26 WEDNESDAY   *Moon Age Day 5 • Moon Sign Libra*

am ....

pm ....
You could find that although most of the people you come across are
extremely supportive at present, there are one or two people who remain
determined to be awkward. Instead of meeting them head on you would
be better advised to take a slight detour yourself.

27 THURSDAY   *Moon Age Day 6 • Moon Sign Libra*

am ....

pm ....
With the lunar low now around you cannot expect to make the sort of
progress that has been more than possible at other stages this month.
The present trend does not last long and does at least offer you the chance
to sit back and take stock of matters before acting positively later.

28 FRIDAY
Moon Age Day 7 • Moon Sign Scorpio

am ....

pm ....
Minor personal disappointments are soon going to pass and are not really worth the sort of attention that you might be inclined to give them. Probably not a good time for spending more money than you have to and certainly an ideal period for pacing yourself when it comes to work.

29 SATURDAY
Moon Age Day 8 • Moon Sign Scorpio

am ....

pm ....
Although you should find yourself making up your mind concerning certain personal issues, you are still not exactly on top form when it comes to getting what you truly want from life. As a result you may tend to hang back in the shadows, a position from which you can achieved very little.

30 SUNDAY
Moon Age Day 9 • Moon Sign Sagittarius

am ....

pm ....
Let your partner, or loved ones, into your secrets. It is more than possible that they already know the way your mind is working but if this is not the case you will need to enlist their support. Keeping people in the dark concerning almost any situation is not recommended for today.

← *NEGATIVE TREND*						*POSITIVE TREND* →				
-5	-4	-3	-2	-1	**LOVE**	+1	+2	+3	+4	+5
					MONEY					
					LUCK					
					VITALITY					

31 MONDAY
Moon Age Day 10 • Moon Sign Sagittarius

am . . . .

pm . . . .
You are the receiver of much goodwill at present and tend to push your own positive nature forward as a result. Life should be looking smoother and there are less obstacles about than might have been the case for the last week or two. Financial advantages could soon be on offer.

1 TUESDAY
Moon Age Day 11 • Moon Sign Sagittarius

am . . . .

pm . . . .
It is true that you tend to take a very philosophical view of life today and that means that you probably get minor problems out of the way very quickly indeed. It might not be exactly easy living up to your own expectations of yourself but the effort proves to be more than worthwhile eventually.

2 WEDNESDAY
Moon Age Day 12 • Moon Sign Capricorn

am . . . .

pm . . . .
Others could find you to be rather erratic and more than a little temperamental at the moment, which is why you might have to modify your ideas and opinions during the day. A good time for romance, and better still if you keep your eyes and ears open. Routines are a chore and mostly you can't be bothered.

3 THURSDAY
Moon Age Day 13 • Moon Sign Capricorn

am . . . .

pm . . . .
Professional developments are both surprising and useful. Any sort of difficulty that you come across early in the day tends to be dealt with efficiently and calmly, though the same cannot be said for personal issues, which find you erratic and less than willing to co-operate,

4 FRIDAY
Moon Age Day 14 • Moon Sign Aquarius

am ....

pm ....
It may be rather difficult to know exactly where you stand in an emotional sense and this is something of an overhang from yesterday. Be willing to talk and to put your point of view in a reasoned manner and you cannot really go wrong. Possibly a good day for any form of travel.

5 SATURDAY
Moon Age Day 15 • Moon Sign Aquarius

am ....

pm ....
The weekend finds you in the mood to tackle career issues, which could be a little difficult if you are at home for Saturday and Sunday. Nevertheless you are able to get your head around issues that have been bothering you for a while and should find the day to be generally useful.

6 SUNDAY
Moon Age Day 16 • Moon Sign Pisces

am ....

pm ....
The sky looks brighter and life is more interesting now, thanks to the present position of Venus in your solar chart. The main sphere of influence is associated with personal relationships, which now take on a much more comfortable feel than was possible in previous days.

	← NEGATIVE TREND						POSITIVE TREND →				
-5	-4	-3	-2	-1			+1	+2	+3	+4	+5
					LOVE						
					MONEY						
					LUCK						
					VITALITY						

YOUR MONTH AT A GLANCE

The twelve numbered boxes represent the important areas in your life. The key to the numbers you will find beneath the panel. A sun above the number indicates that opportunities are around. A cloud below the number, that you should be a bit defensive. Nothing above or below and life will be pretty ordinary.

					☀				☀		☀
1	**2**	**3**	**4**	**5**	**6**	**7**	**8**	**9**	**10**	**11**	**12**
						☁	☁				

KEY

1 Strength of Personality
2 Personal Finance
3 Useful Information Gathering
4 Domestic Affairs
5 Pleasure & Romance
6 Effective Work & Health

7 One to One Relationships
8 Questioning, Thinking & Deciding
9 External Influences / Education
10 Career Aspirations
11 Teamwork Activities
12 Unconscious Impulses

SEPTEMBER HIGHS AND LOWS

Here, I show how the rhythm of the Moon will affect you this month. Like the tide, your energies and abilities will rise and fall with its pattern. When it is above the date line, go-for-it. When it is below the line you should be resting.

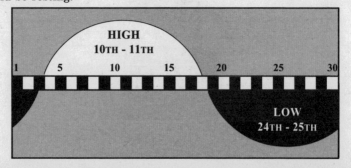

7 MONDAY   *Moon Age Day 17 • Moon Sign Pisces*

am . . . .

pm . . . .

It is possible that you will find it rather difficult to compromise today and will need to be on your best behaviour if you really want to get the very best from any given situation. The problem seems to be that there is a little of Taurean stubborn quality showing through for a day or two.

8 TUESDAY   *Moon Age Day 18 • Moon Sign Aries*

am . . . .

pm . . . .

The more you manage to get done today, the less you will find yourself having to deal with later in the week, which considering all that you want to deal with at that time would turn out to be a very good thing. Aside from this fact you are clearly on a roll at the moment and proving difficult to beat.

9 WEDNESDAY   *Moon Age Day 19 • Moon Sign Aries*

am . . . .

pm . . . .

You could quite easily find yourself being led up the garden path today, which is not an ideal situation. This is far less likely if you keep your wits about you and if you judge any offer as being rather suspect until you have had the chance to look at it properly. Slight hitches are soon sorted out however.

10 THURSDAY   *Moon Age Day 20 • Moon Sign Taurus*

am . . . .

pm . . . .

The Moon is back in your sign and brings an interlude that should appear to be far less complicated than what has been on offer for the last few days. You are free to choose whatever path suits you the best and suffer less from fatigue and general self-doubts of a dubious sort.

149

11 FRIDAY

Moon Age Day 21 • Moon Sign Taurus

am . . . .

pm . . . .

Keep up the good work. There are no shortage of new projects in the offing and plenty to play for during the days that lie ahead. Much of the success starts here and comes thanks to a very positive attitude on your part. Putting yourself to the test only proves how capable you can be.

12 SATURDAY

Moon Age Day 22 • Moon Sign Gemini

am . . . .

pm . . . .

Though you are anxious to maintain a degree of financial stability in your life it might be necessary to take some fairly radical action that will make the situation look worse before it gets better. Short-term action is very necessary but does turn out to be for the best when viewed later.

13 SUNDAY

Moon Age Day 23 • Moon Sign Gemini

am . . . .

pm . . . .

Whilst there is much emphasis being placed on pleasure at the moment, it is obvious that you still feel yourself to be fairly busy in a practical sense. Balancing the two opposing needs may not be all that easy, but if you also rely on the advice of a loved one you probably won't go far wrong.

← NEGATIVE TREND							POSITIVE TREND →			
-5	-4	-3	-2	-1			+1	+2	+3	+4	+5
					LOVE						
					MONEY						
					LUCK						
					VITALITY						

14 MONDAY
Moon Age Day 24 • Moon Sign Cancer

am ....

pm ....
There is much to-ing and fro-ing to be dealt with at the start of this
working week, and that means having to balance a certain amount of
activity early in the day. You are being called upon for help and advice
and will be doing all you can to answer every type of need that arises.

15 TUESDAY
Moon Age Day 25 • Moon Sign Cancer

am ....

pm ....
Positive trends still surround your life in terms of romance and pleasure
and you should be feeling well on form. Anxiety tends to be for the birds
and you should not allow small niggles to get in the way. Personality
wise you are certainly making a favourable impression on almost
everyone.

16 WEDNESDAY
Moon Age Day 26 • Moon Sign Cancer

am ....

pm ....
If you are to serve the needs of society as much as you might, you first
of all need to ensure that your own life is taking the course that you would
wish it to. As usual you are brave and able to make the most of a personal
offer that means going slightly out on a limb. Romance remains positive.

17 THURSDAY
Moon Age Day 27 • Moon Sign Leo

am ....

pm ....
A family member or a good friend may attempt to force you into some
mode of action that is certainly not of your own choosing. The only way
that you can deal with this situation is to make it plain that you will not
be altered in your opinions. You may not be too popular for a few hours
though.

18 FRIDAY

Moon Age Day 28 • Moon Sign Leo

am ....

pm ....

Although you manage to elicit a positive action from most other people today, your own attitudes tend to be rather more pessimistic. There is no real reason for this state of affairs, apart from the fact that you have got yourself into a particular way of thinking that is not especially useful.

19 SATURDAY

Moon Age Day 29 • Moon Sign Virgo

am ....

pm ....

There is never a dull moment for Taurus today and it is clear that much has changed since yesterday. A generally bright and breezy sort of attitude on your part lifts the quality of almost any situation and certainly makes you fun to have around. Happiness comes as a natural consequence.

20 SUNDAY

Moon Age Day 0 • Moon Sign Virgo

am ....

pm ....

Get out of the house today if it proves to be at all possible to do so. You need fresh fields and pastures new in order to stimulate your mind into working in new directions. Some doubts about a project that you have recently taken on are not really necessary because you have covered all possibilities.

← NEGATIVE TREND						POSITIVE TREND →				
-5	-4	-3	-2	-1		+1	+2	+3	+4	+5
					LOVE					
					MONEY					
					LUCK					
					VITALITY					

21 MONDAY
Moon Age Day 1 • Moon Sign Libra

am ....

pm ....
You may not be too certain of yourself today and that means having to
check your facts before you push forward into unknown territory. In a
personal sense you are very good to know and you are more than willing
to put yourself out to help almost anyone. Love matters take a surprising
turn.

22 TUESDAY
Moon Age Day 2 • Moon Sign Libra

am ....

pm ....
It may not appear so early in the day but this could turn out to be one of
the most successful periods in the month. The main reason for the
possible gains is that you are now certainly not hiding your light under
a bushel. You know what you are capable of and are quite willing to be
bold.

23 WEDNESDAY
Moon Age Day 3 • Moon Sign Libra

am ....

pm ....
Things are bound to slow a little towards the end of today as the Moon
enters your opposite sign. This time around the happening may not
prove all that noticeable but it does at least offer a few moments now and
again to think matters through carefully. Friends take some of the
strain.

24 THURSDAY
Moon Age Day 4 • Moon Sign Scorpio

am ....

pm ....
A little solitude is something that you may deliberately opt for today.
There are times when all Taureans need to charge their batteries and
since you cannot make startling progress at present this may well be
used as one of them. However, little should hold you back personally
speaking.

25 FRIDAY

Moon Age Day 5 • Moon Sign Scorpio

am . . . .

pm . . . .
Although the Moon is still in Scorpio it should seem as if most aspects of
your life are starting to gain a little more momentum. Don't allow
yourself to be browbeaten into any sort of practical action that you know
to be silly and gradually increase your influence with others as the day
advances.

26 SATURDAY

Moon Age Day 6 • Moon Sign Sagittarius

am . . . .

pm . . . .
Love and romance are especially well highlighted today and this is the
sphere of life that you are likely to be looking at most closely right now.
You tend to be very active on the home front and might be deciding that
this is the time to change your surroundings in a rather big way.

27 SUNDAY

Moon Age Day 7 • Moon Sign Sagittarius

am . . . .

pm . . . .
You definitely have the wherewithal to make fundamental alterations to
your plans. All the same, this ability is no use unless you have thought
matters through very carefully and that is what today is all about.
Meanwhile you can expect some compliments from family members and
friends.

← *NEGATIVE TREND*						*POSITIVE TREND* →				
-5	-4	-3	-2	-1		+1	+2	+3	+4	+5
					LOVE					
					MONEY					
					LUCK					
					VITALITY					

28 MONDAY
Moon Age Day 8 • Moon Sign Sagittarius

am ....

pm ....
With hardly a minute to yourself and everything to play for at work, you are probably on the go from the very moment that the cock crows. Stand by an opinion that you arrived at a few days ago, though do be prepared to modify your stance over personal matters if it proves to be necessary.

29 TUESDAY
Moon Age Day 9 • Moon Sign Capricorn

am ....

pm ....
With a little more free time likely today you do at least have the chance of pleasing yourself a little. Of course much depends on your own attitude because if you have got it into your head that you are indispensable, then you will carry on regardless and might miss some of the fun.

30 WEDNESDAY
Moon Age Day 10 • Moon Sign Capricorn

am ....

pm ....
Progress at work is at least steady and there seems little that should get in your way right now. Routines don't really suit you at present, but you find ways and means to get round them all the same. Look out for some loving messages and respond to them in the same positive tones.

1 THURSDAY
Moon Age Day 11 • Moon Sign Aquarius

am ....

pm ....
Professional developments look possible, but you will have to keep your eyes open if you want to make the very best out of what they are offering. Confidence tends to be fairly high and there is support of a personal nature coming from what might turn out to be the most unlikely direction.

2 FRIDAY

Moon Age Day 12 • Moon Sign Aquarius

am...

pm...
Although you sense a few limitations in your life, these should do little to prevent progress that looks good in most areas. Allow matters to develop as they must and avoid interfering in situations that show a tendency to sort themselves out. A friend in need could divert your attention at some stage.

3 SATURDAY

Moon Age Day 13 • Moon Sign Pisces

am...

pm...
Group and teamwork possibilities find you using the weekend for projects that you may not have planned in advance. Try to stay away from squabbles that cannot assist you in any way and if necessary keep to your own council. This might not be easy if friends are rowing in your vicinity.

4 SUNDAY

Moon Age Day 14 • Moon Sign Pisces

am...

pm...
If there is any conflict about today it tends to show itself on the home front. Once again the advice for you is to stay away from it if you possibly can. You are not going to gain anything from being forced to take a particular point of view at a time when flexibility is more likely to be the key.

← *NEGATIVE TREND*					*POSITIVE TREND* →				
-5	-4	-3	-2	-1	+1	+2	+3	+4	+5
					LOVE				
					MONEY				
					LUCK				
					VITALITY				

1998

YOUR MONTH AT A GLANCE

The twelve numbered boxes represent the important areas in your life. The key to the numbers you will find beneath the panel. A sun above the number indicates that opportunities are around. A cloud below the number, that you should be a bit defensive. Nothing above or below and life will be pretty ordinary.

1	2	3	4	5	6	7	8	9	10	11	12

KEY

1 Strength of Personality	7 One to One Relationships
2 Personal Finance	8 Questioning, Thinking & Deciding
3 Useful Information Gathering	9 External Influences / Education
4 Domestic Affairs	10 Career Aspirations
5 Pleasure & Romance	11 Teamwork Activities
6 Effective Work & Health	12 Unconscious Impulses

OCTOBER HIGHS AND LOWS

Here, I show how the rhythm of the Moon will affect you this month. Like the tide, your energies and abilities will rise and fall with its pattern. When it is above the date line, go-for-it. When it is below the line you should be resting.

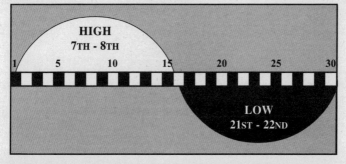

5 MONDAY

Moon Age Day 15 • Moon Sign Aries

am ....

pm ....
Practical matters take up much of your time today and probably leave
you with few hours to explore the more personal aspects of your life. Still
you should find that by the end of the day it has proved possible to make
more real progress than has been the case for quite a number of days.

6 TUESDAY

Moon Age Day 16 • Moon Sign Aries

am ....

pm ....
Before today is out you should notice the more positive aspects being
brought into your life by the position of the Moon, which should be in a
very real position to help you out this time around. A day to plan, ahead
of great activity later in the week. Keep plodding away steadily however.

7 WEDNESDAY

Moon Age Day 17 • Moon Sign Taurus

am ....

pm ....
The lunar high should lift the middle of the week clear out of the
ordinary, even if this comes about in fairly expected ways at first. Life
throws a number of surprises into your path and it would be sensible to
take most of them at face value. A time to accept and not one in which
to tinker.

8 THURSDAY

Moon Age Day 18 • Moon Sign Taurus

am ....

pm ....
Whatever you are wanting from life, you now find yourself in a stage
where it is possible to get it. If you have been waiting for a suitable
opportunity to put a much thought about plan into action, this is the
time. Only Taureans who hold back will be left at the starting blocks
right now.

9 FRIDAY
Moon Age Day 19 • Moon Sign Gemini

am ....

pm ....
Maintaining the momentum that you have built up across the preceding days is not going to be easy, but it is nearly the end of the working week for most of you, and it could count as an ideal time to tie up all the loose ends that you activities have created. You will not be lethargic however.

10 SATURDAY
Moon Age Day 20 • Moon Sign Gemini

am ....

pm ....
Whilst the present association of Mars and Saturn is not negative, it probably isn't all that helpful either. Some of your expectations, especially at a personal level, may not turn out quite as you might have imagined and you will have to be both inventive and flexible to make headway now.

11 SUNDAY
Moon Age Day 21 • Moon Sign Gemini

am ....

pm ....
A good day for gathering information, ahead of definite pushes that come with the working week. You may decide to potter in the garden today, or to simply do things around the house. A fairly uneventful day that could show itself as having been very useful in the fullness of time.

← NEGATIVE TREND						POSITIVE TREND →				
-5	-4	-3	-2	-1		+1	+2	+3	+4	+5
					LOVE					
					MONEY					
					LUCK					
					VITALITY					

12 MONDAY
Moon Age Day 22 • Moon Sign Cancer

am ....

pm ....
Social matters are a source of happiness, even if more practical considerations are out of the window for a short while. There is everything to play for in the romantic stakes and you might find yourself more than bowled over by the reactions and compliments coming from a loved one.

13 TUESDAY
Moon Age Day 23 • Moon Sign Cancer

am ....

pm ....
There are some potentially good trends around today, but the word of caution is that you should not allow yourself to take too many decisions for the long-term future. As long as you recognise the most positive sphere of influence as being today, then you cannot go far wrong.

14 WEDNESDAY
Moon Age Day 24 • Moon Sign Leo

am ....

pm ....
A little less focused than might normally be the case, you would do well today to check out your potential schemes with someone who is very close to you. It is likely that the fact that they are not personally involved allows them a perspective that is missing from your own life right now.

15 THURSDAY
Moon Age Day 25 • Moon Sign Leo

am ....

pm ....
An excellent period in which to bring about changes to your working environment. There are some very useful people around at the present time and you should not underestimate the potential that they have for making the right decisions on your behalf. Love deepens later in the day.

16 FRIDAY
Moon Age Day 26 • Moon Sign Virgo

am . . . .

pm . . . .
Although it might be something of a problem to bring others round to your own point of view today, you can achieve this objective with just a little concentration. Once you have made up your mind to any particular course of action it would be sensible not to change it again later in the day.

17 SATURDAY
Moon Age Day 27 • Moon Sign Virgo

am . . . .

pm . . . .
There seems to be an emphasis on your more gentle side today and you should also find that the Taurean creative streak is very noticeable. Someone you have not seen for quite a while could be making an renewed entry into your life and bringing a surprise or two along with them.

18 SUNDAY
Moon Age Day 28 • Moon Sign Virgo

am . . . .

pm . . . .
Your social life is likely to remain fairly busy today and there are not many moments that you could actually call your own. Perhaps you had better take yourself off to a quiet spot at some stage however because there are certain questions in your mind that deserve a considered answer.

← NEGATIVE TREND						POSITIVE TREND →				
-5	-4	-3	-2	-1		+1	+2	+3	+4	+5
					LOVE					
					MONEY					
					LUCK					
					VITALITY					

161

19 MONDAY
Moon Age Day 29 • Moon Sign Libra

am ....

pm ....
Others may be expecting you to do more for them than seems reasonable
to you, which is why you have to split your time just as carefully as you
can today. In the end you should be able to fit everything in, though not
without something of a struggle. A little prior planning would probably
help.

20 TUESDAY
Moon Age Day 0 • Moon Sign Libra

am ....

pm ....
A time when you definitely need to be more motivated than might have
been possible recently. Of course it is not easy to get yourself into this
frame of mind simply by wishing that it was so, though you do have
tremendous reserves of energy to call on if it really proves to be
necessary.

21 WEDNESDAY
Moon Age Day 1 • Moon Sign Scorpio

am ....

pm ....
The lunar low slows things down a little but probably not as much as you
would normally expect. If you have been wise and watching events you
will already have off loaded some of your more pressing responsibilities
onto other people. This will leave you free to look at personal matters.

22 THURSDAY
Moon Age Day 2 • Moon Sign Scorpio

am ....

pm ....
Once again you find yourself a little restricted by circumstance. This
could prove to be rather frustrating at this time of the week and if certain
matters have to be put on hold, leave them in a state which means quick
action later. Anxiety is not very likely, and certainly not useful.

23 FRIDAY   *Moon Age Day 3 • Moon Sign Scorpio*

am..

pm..
The Sun enters your solar seventh house, bringing you into a period
when you are looking closely at one to one relationships. You could be
looking again at your recent attitudes and deciding that a modification
is necessary. Don't rush though because you have a month or so to act.

24 SATURDAY   *Moon Age Day 4 • Moon Sign Sagittarius*

am..

pm..
A bright and happy time comes along and there is plenty to keep you both
happy and occupied at the moment. Routines are for the birds and you
should breeze through most tasks without even recognising that you
have been busy with them. Romance plays a significant part in your
weekend.

25 SUNDAY   *Moon Age Day 5 • Moon Sign Sagittarius*

am..

pm..
Don't hang back when discussions are taking place, especially when you
know that your involvement now can mean an easier time in the longer
term. A brave side to your nature makes you willing to speak out, even
when other people appear to know their ground better than you.

← NEGATIVE TREND						POSITIVE TREND →				
-5	-4	-3	-2	-1		+1	+2	+3	+4	+5
					LOVE					
					MONEY					
					LUCK					
					VITALITY					

26 MONDAY
Moon Age Day 6 • Moon Sign Capricorn

am ....

pm ....
Opt for a change to your everyday routines at the start of this working
week and be willing to listen to what colleagues and friends have to say.
There is a dreamy side to your nature at present and you need to take
a little time to allow the dreams to play themselves out.

27 TUESDAY
Moon Age Day 7 • Moon Sign Capricorn

am ....

pm ....
The possibilities of your social life should bring a smile to your face and
make it possible to ring the changes in ways that might have seemed less
than likely only a short time ago. Everybody you meet has something
interesting to say and you can gain much simply by listening.

28 WEDNESDAY
Moon Age Day 8 • Moon Sign Capricorn

am ....

pm ....
If there is any pressure about today you don't need to respond to it more
than is strictly necessary. A deeply felt air of excitement is difficult to
understand, but is certain to herald some fairly positive events not so far
down the line. With a particular objective in mind, push forward.

29 THURSDAY
Moon Age Day 9 • Moon Sign Aquarius

am ....

pm ....
There is much emphasis now on simply having fun. Although the
general pressures of the day do have to be dealt with, at the same time
all work and no play is not at all good for you. Even getting your practical
head to work properly can be difficult, not that you really care at present.

30 FRIDAY
Moon Age Day 10 • Moon Sign Aquarius

am ....

pm ....
There is an element of power play evident within personal relationships, though of course you don't have to respond and certainly are not forced into arguments, which would not help anything at the moment. Keep a sense of proportion and avoid being pushed into confusing situations.

31 SATURDAY
Moon Age Day 11 • Moon Sign Pisces

am ....

pm ....
Keeping up a high social profile is not really all that difficult, and the weekend offers you the chance to mix with all sorts of interesting and stimulating types. There might be a slight tendency to feel threatened personally, but there is no real reason to take notice of this peculiarity.

1 SUNDAY
Moon Age Day 12 • Moon Sign Pisces

am ....

pm ....
You will be amazed at just how much you can get done, even if you don't exactly make a startling commencement to the day. Slow and steady is the recipe and the finished creation is quite spectacular. By the evening you should be quite happy to take a little rest however.

← *NEGATIVE TREND*						*POSITIVE TREND* →				
-5	-4	-3	-2	-1	LOVE	+1	+2	+3	+4	+5
					MONEY					
					LUCK					
					VITALITY					

YOUR MONTH AT A GLANCE

The twelve numbered boxes represent the important areas in your life. The key to the numbers you will find beneath the panel. A sun above the number indicates that opportunities are around. A cloud below the number, that you should be a bit defensive. Nothing above or below and life will be pretty ordinary.

1	2	3	4	5	6	7	8	9	10	11	12

KEY

1 Strength of Personality
2 Personal Finance
3 Useful Information Gathering
4 Domestic Affairs
5 Pleasure & Romance
6 Effective Work & Health

7 One to One Relationships
8 Questioning, Thinking & Deciding
9 External Influences / Education
10 Career Aspirations
11 Teamwork Activities
12 Unconscious Impulses

NOVEMBER HIGHS AND LOWS

Here, I show how the rhythm of the Moon will affect you this month. Like the tide, your energies and abilities will rise and fall with its pattern. When it is above the date line, go-for-it. When it is below the line you should be resting.

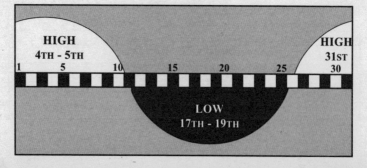

2 MONDAY   *Moon Age Day 13 • Moon Sign Aries*

am ....

pm ....
A friend or perhaps a colleague has something very important to tell you,
so you had better be in a position to listen carefully when the time comes.
Attention to details is essential at all stages today because there are
many small gains to be made if you keep your wits about you.

3 TUESDAY   *Moon Age Day 14 • Moon Sign Aries*

am ....

pm ....
Later in the day the Moon returns to Taurus and brings with it a very
positive phase for most of you. Things probably will not start out that
way however and you could be wondering exactly what you have to do to
get life going your way at first. Patience Taurus. Things soon come good.

4 WEDNESDAY   *Moon Age Day 15 • Moon Sign Taurus*

am ....

pm ....
Climb aboard the roller coaster of life and enjoy the ride that you could
so easily undertake at this time. If, on the other hand, you decide to stay
quietly in the background, you could find that you are missing out on
some very special opportunities. All possibilities are grist to the mill
now.

5 THURSDAY   *Moon Age Day 16 • Moon Sign Taurus*

am ....

pm ....
Things continue to work well for you and there is no reason at all why you
should not find yourself in a stronger position than at any other stage
this month. Personality clashes are just possible if you allow the more
positive side of your nature to run away with you, so tact is important.

6 FRIDAY
Moon Age Day 17 • Moon Sign Gemini

am . . . .

pm . . . .
Goodwill coming from the direction of relatives and friends is more than
welcome, and arrives in part thanks to the effort that you have put in on
their behalf earlier on. Social impulses are strong and it is likely that you
will be out in the midst of any activity life chooses to throw in your
direction.

7 SATURDAY
Moon Age Day 18 • Moon Sign Gemini

am . . . .

pm . . . .
Stuck between the need for leisure and the desire to keep going at all
cost, you are more than capable of wearing yourself out. Not everyone
understands the way that your mind is working and it could be good to
make certain that you have moments to spare to explain yourself fully.

8 SUNDAY
Moon Age Day 19 • Moon Sign Cancer

am . . . .

pm . . . .
Once again on the go from the very start, you make yourself indispensa-
ble to just about everyone. Probably a good day for a small wager but not
a time to lay your shirt on the line without thinking very carefully first.
Old, unusual or curious things have a real fascination for you now.

← *NEGATIVE TREND*								*POSITIVE TREND* →				
-5	-4	-3	-2	-1				+1	+2	+3	+4	+5
					LOVE							
					MONEY							
					LUCK							
					VITALITY							

9 MONDAY   *Moon Age Day 20 • Moon Sign Cancer*

am . . . .

pm . . . .

It's time to feel good about yourself. This may not be as easy as it first appears, especially if certain people seem to fail to recognise the potential that you have. In truth they probably realise all too well, but might be too embarrassed or shy to tell you how they are really feeling.

10 TUESDAY   *Moon Age Day 21 • Moon Sign Leo*

am . . . .

pm . . . .

You are now likely to be taking a more prominent roll in a dozen situations which had little or no part to play in your life previously. Balancing all the various potentials that stand around you now is not going to be all that easy. Relations and good friends hold the key to your choices.

11 WEDNESDAY   *Moon Age Day 22 • Moon Sign Leo*

am . . . .

pm . . . .

There is likely to be be some conflict between domestic needs and the desire that you have to please yourself at the moment. A sensible balance is possible and will be achieved if you only split your time carefully. Later in the day the social possibilities tend to attract you the most.

12 THURSDAY   *Moon Age Day 23 • Moon Sign Virgo*

am . . . .

pm . . . .

It is possible that you may be a little suspicious regarding the motives of a colleague or friend. You have great intuition to rely on however and can rely on your own judgement, no matter what others may have to say about the situation. A good time to read or even to jot down your own thoughts.

13 FRIDAY
Moon Age Day 24 • Moon Sign Virgo

am . . . .

pm . . . .
Romantic issues may be uppermost in your mind at present and if you are not attached, the chance is that there is some offer coming your way around now. People seem to recognise the best of what you are and it is to be hoped that their opinions rub off on you too. Avoid confusion in friendships.

14 SATURDAY
Moon Age Day 25 • Moon Sign Virgo

am . . . .

pm . . . .
An excellent boost to all relationships, personal or more distant, and the chance to do whatever takes your fancy. If the weekend means being at home, you may decide to curl up by the fire and this is probably the best place to be. Later in the day there could be some surprises.

15 SUNDAY
Moon Age Day 26 • Moon Sign Libra

am . . . .

pm . . . .
Despite the many ups and downs that life has to offer you, you should be busy and contented this Sunday. Any financial gains that comes your way are likely to be fairly small, but welcome all the same. The best gifts that life offers come from friends of whom you are especially fond.

←	*NEGATIVE TREND*						*POSITIVE TREND*		→	
-5	-4	-3	-2	-1		+1	+2	+3	+4	+5
					LOVE					
					MONEY					
					LUCK					
					VITALITY					

16 MONDAY   *Moon Age Day 27 • Moon Sign Libra*

am ....

pm ....
You could easily feel quite restless at the start of this working week and
will need to keep yourself busy until the mood passes. Acting on impulse
is fine, but may not work so well when money is involved. Financial
decisions should probably wait until after the middle of the week.

17 TUESDAY   *Moon Age Day 28 • Moon Sign Scorpio*

am ....

pm ....
The lunar low might make for a quiet spell, but that does not mean that
you fail to gain anything from the period. On the whole you should feel
fairly secure and generally content with your lot, even if life is not as busy
as you would wish. Time spent alone is not at all wasted.

18 WEDNESDAY   *Moon Age Day 29 • Moon Sign Scorpio*

am ....

pm ....
There is some good luck about at the moment, even if it takes a while
before you get round to recognising the fact. Staying away from noisy or
disruptive types comes more or less as second nature and you are likely
to be pleased with yourself for a variety of different reasons.

19 THURSDAY   *Moon Age Day 0 • Moon Sign Scorpio*

am ....

pm ....
The potential of personal challenges is what sets this day apart, probably
from the very start. A warm welcome awaits you in any new situation
and there are people around who should fascinate you. A good time for
solving puzzles and for coming to terms with situations from the past.

20 FRIDAY
Moon Age Day 1 • Moon Sign Sagittarius

am ....

pm ....
Any changes you want to make to your personal world at the moment tend to be very small in scale but could have far greater repercussions in the fullness of time. The end of the working week brings a new way of thinking and the chance to ring the changes in all social situations.

21 SATURDAY
♦ *Moon Age Day 2 • Moon Sign Sagittarius*

am ....

pm ....
Others have the ability to put a stop to your own personal desires, or at least that may be what they are thinking. It wouldn't really help anything to tell them different and in any case you can achieve much more by simply carrying on in your own sweet way. Quiet Taurus is most effective now.

22 SUNDAY
♦ *Moon Age Day 3 • Moon Sign Capricorn*

am ....

pm ....
A period of breakdown and renewal is evident, and indeed may have been so for some days now. Coming to terms with this fact is essential if you are to make the most of all that is on offer. The remainder of November demands a greater input, but the rewards are well worth the effort.

	← NEGATIVE TREND						POSITIVE TREND →				
	-5	-4	-3	-2	-1		+1	+2	+3	+4	+5
LOVE											
MONEY											
LUCK											
VITALITY											

23 MONDAY ♦ *Moon Age Day 4 • Moon Sign Capricorn*

am..

pm..

Personal freedom beckons, and you probably take the chance to go wherever the sign posts are pointing. Making up your mind to follow your own ideas may not be too easy, but once you have set out on the journey, there is very little chance to retrace your steps. Happiness seems to beckon.

24 TUESDAY ♦ *Moon Age Day 5 • Moon Sign Capricorn*

am..

pm..

Gains come from some fairly unexpected directions at present and you should be out there in the mainstream of life having a really good time. There are few errors of judgement around and a great desire to mix with groups or associations that have not played a part in your life before.

25 WEDNESDAY ♦ *Moon Age Day 6 • Moon Sign Aquarius*

am..

pm..

Getting to a solution for any minor difficulty is not too awkward now. In addition to your own common sense there are people around who are more than willing to offer support and good advice. Friends could turn out to be more reliable than relatives at present, mainly because they are detached.

26 THURSDAY ♦ *Moon Age Day 7 • Moon Sign Aquarius*

am..

pm..

Your very best moments today are likely to be those spent in the company of people whom you love. Personal relationships are looking especially good and you find that you have much more in common with one or two people than you have come to believe. Surprises are inevitable.

27 FRIDAY
♦ *Moon Age Day 8 • Moon Sign Pisces*

am ....

pm ....
There are challenges about today, but few of them are of a nature that would worry you in any way. You love the cut and thrust of everyday life and are likely to find yourself thrust into the midst of any situation that baffles others. Intimate relationships are still looking very pleasant.

28 SATURDAY
♦ *Moon Age Day 9 • Moon Sign Pisces*

am ....

pm ....
It might be best to do things alone today, and especially so if you want to get them done as quickly as possible. There is time to fit in most of the tasks that you are determined to set yourself but it is important not to be so busy that you fail to recognise less practical gains that arise.

29 SUNDAY
♦ *Moon Age Day 10 • Moon Sign Aries*

am ....

pm ....
For the first time in a number of weeks your love life could turn out to be a little tricky at the moment. To side-step the possibility you might decide to keep yourself busy with matters that play no part in your personal life. Changes in and around your home may once again become important.

← *NEGATIVE TREND*						*POSITIVE TREND* →				
-5	-4	-3	-2	-1		+1	+2	+3	+4	+5
					LOVE					
					MONEY					
					LUCK					
					VITALITY					

30 MONDAY ♦ *Moon Age Day 11 • Moon Sign Aries*

am ....

pm ....
Don't believe everything that you are told today. Although it is not likely that people are deliberately trying to pull the wool over your eyes, they too may be confused. Join them in a quest to discover the truth and you may even make some important new friends whilst you are at it.

1 TUESDAY ♦ *Moon Age Day 12 • Moon Sign Taurus*

am ....

pm ....
Fortunate times are on the way as the Moons speeds back into your sign. There is everything to play for, and although today might find you rather busy, you should still be able to find enough time to please yourself once the practical parts of the day are over and done with.

2 WEDNESDAY ♦ *Moon Age Day 13 • Moon Sign Taurus*

am ....

pm ....
A day for making some important decisions, not least of all financial ones. You can probably afford to push your luck a little and might even be deciding that the time is right for a change of job or responsibility. Concern for a family member is quite probably misplaced at this time.

3 THURSDAY ♦ *Moon Age Day 14 • Moon Sign Taurus*

am ....

pm ....
The Moon hangs in your sign, allowing a fairly positive start to the working day. If you have a few hours to yourself this would be a very good time for travelling, but you won't want to be doing it on your own. Get to grips with a home based issue that might have been playing on your mind.

4 FRIDAY ♦ *Moon Age Day 15 • Moon Sign Gemini*

am...

pm...
Positive influences have a part to play in your personal life and make the immediate future look fairly bright. There could be one or two little tasks to get out of the way at work ahead of the weekend and you will be anxious to make just as much out of your social life as you can.

5 SATURDAY ♦ *Moon Age Day 16 • Moon Sign Gemini*

am...

pm...
The weekend offers some new incentives and a very different way of looking at everyday problems. Progress is possible on most fronts and you should find yourself with a great deal more energy to spare than might usually be the case by the weekend. A good time to start an adventure.

6 SUNDAY ♦ *Moon Age Day 17 • Moon Sign Cancer*

am...

pm...
If instant decisions are called for there is no point at all in jumping around from foot to foot. Try to be as sure of yourself as other people seem to think that you are and be prepared to spend some time sorting out details before you plunge headlong into situations that could be confusing.

← NEGATIVE TREND						POSITIVE TREND →				
-5	-4	-3	-2	-1		+1	+2	+3	+4	+5
					LOVE					
					MONEY					
					LUCK					
					VITALITY					

1998

YOUR MONTH AT A GLANCE

The twelve numbered boxes represent the important areas in your life. The key to the numbers you will find beneath the panel. A sun above the number indicates that opportunities are around. A cloud below the number, that you should be a bit defensive. Nothing above or below and life will be pretty ordinary.

1	2	3	4	5	6	7	8	9	10	11	12

KEY

1 Strength of Personality
2 Personal Finance
3 Useful Information Gathering
4 Domestic Affairs
5 Pleasure & Romance
6 Effective Work & Health

7 One to One Relationships
8 Questioning, Thinking & Deciding
9 External Influences / Education
10 Career Aspirations
11 Teamwork Activities
12 Unconscious Impulses

DECEMBER HIGHS AND LOWS

Here, I show how the rhythm of the Moon will affect you this month. Like the tide, your energies and abilities will rise and fall with its pattern. When it is above the date line, go-for-it. When it is below the line you should be resting.

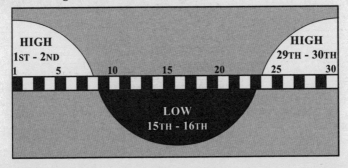

7 MONDAY
♦ *Moon Age Day 18 • Moon Sign Leo*

am..

pm..
The main area of fulfilment in your life at present is likely to be
associated with your home and family. Things may not be running quite
as smoothly at work as you could wish, but this situation will turn itself
around before the month is very much older. Spend time with family
members.

8 TUESDAY
♦ *Moon Age Day 19 • Moon Sign Leo*

am..

pm..
Certain demands are made of you and there might just be a slight fear
that you are not equal to the task. This is clearly not true because you
are adaptable and hard working right now. Trying to persuade yourself
of your real talents isn't easy today, but may turn out to be very
necessary.

9 WEDNESDAY
♦ *Moon Age Day 20 • Moon Sign Leo*

am..

pm..
Emotional intimacy now becomes possible and more likely. The warmer
side of Taurus begins to show itself more fully and you are definitely at
the head of the queue when it comes to receiving compliments. Even
people who have disagreed with you in the past are more reasonable
now.

10 THURSDAY
♦ *Moon Age Day 21 • Moon Sign Virgo*

am..

pm..
Keep as much as possible to tried and tested methods today for the best
chance of success in the end. Many of the successes you are looking for
will not find you today, but as long as you know that you are on the right
path, everything should come good eventually. A day to speak your
mind.

11 FRIDAY
Moon Age Day 22 • Moon Sign Virgo

am . . . .

pm . . . .
Present planetary influences tend to make social possibilities that much better and you might find that the end of the working week brings a little surprise regarding your profession. Stand up for what you believe to be true in a personal sense but do so in the tried and tested way of the diplomatic Taurean.

12 SATURDAY
Moon Age Day 23 • Moon Sign Libra

am . . . .

pm . . . .
It isn't enough to scrape the surface of any situation right now and you are intent on getting to the bottom of everything. This may be a laudable objective but have you really got the time to do so? Perhaps you will have to be a little selective and choose only one or two really important issues.

13 SUNDAY
Moon Age Day 24 • Moon Sign Libra

am . . . .

pm . . . .
A productive sort of day, no matter whether you are at work or relaxing at home. Any sort of reversal in your social life is not going to last all that long, though there are one or two people around who seem determined to be difficult. The best way to deal with them is to refuse to take any notice.

| ← NEGATIVE TREND | | | | | POSITIVE TREND → | | | | |
-5	-4	-3	-2	-1	+1	+2	+3	+4	+5
					LOVE				
					MONEY				
					LUCK				
					VITALITY				

179

14 MONDAY
Moon Age Day 25 • Moon Sign Libra

am ....

pm ....
You might not feel like pushing over any busses today but that does not
mean the progress is impossible. On the contrary, you have plenty of
ability to succeed in a low key sort of way and can influence life greatly,
without having to make a great deal of noise about it..

15 TUESDAY
Moon Age Day 26 • Moon Sign Scorpio

am ....

pm ....
The lunar low is around again and although this may prevent you from
moving forward quite as quickly or effectively as you would wish, it
certainly will not stop you looking ahead. This is a day to plan strategy
for later, but does not respond to sudden actions or any erratic behaviour.

16 WEDNESDAY
Moon Age Day 27 • Moon Sign Scorpio

am ....

pm ....
It is possible that you could make life just a little difficult for others, even
though this is far from what you are intending to do. It might be best to
treat today as a time for resting because any influence you have on
situations is certainly going to be restricted. New friendships are
possible.

17 THURSDAY
Moon Age Day 28 • Moon Sign Sagittarius

am ....

pm ....
With everything to play for, and the Moon now having left your opposite
sign, you are firmly back in gear again and anxious to get get on with all
sorts of projects. It should appear as if the whole world wants to put itself
out to help you and loving friends especially want to be of assistance.

18 FRIDAY
Moon Age Day 29 • Moon Sign Sagittarius

am...

pm...

Although things have been improving, it was probably difficult until today to feel that you have been in a very stable position, especially at work. A great deal of contentment comes your way now and probably leaves you feeling more comfortable than has been possible for some days.

19 SATURDAY
Moon Age Day 0 • Moon Sign Sagittarius

am...

pm...

You should now be firmly in the picture when it comes to the plans of people in your vicinity. Creating space to please yourself emotionally and practically is not difficult and you tend to deal with minor setbacks in an instant. A puzzle from the past could easily be solved once and for all.

20 SUNDAY
Moon Age Day 1 • Moon Sign Capricorn

am...

pm...

A day when you really need to seek out the wild blue yonder. It isn't that you are particularly fanciful and most of your schemes do stand a chance of coming to fruition. Activities of all sorts tend to appeal to you and last minute plans for Christmas are probably on your mind too.

← NEGATIVE TREND								POSITIVE TREND →				
-5	-4	-3	-2	-1		LOVE		+1	+2	+3	+4	+5
						MONEY						
						LUCK						
						VITALITY						

21 MONDAY   *Moon Age Day 2 • Moon Sign Capricorn*

am . . . .

pm . . . .
There is no stopping the sign of Taurus once it gets going and today could well prove to be a maelstrom of activity from start to finish. Not only do you manage to keep busy yourself, but you also find means to involve everyone else in your ferocious assault on outstanding tasks.

22 TUESDAY   *Moon Age Day 3 • Moon Sign Aquarius*

am . . . .

pm . . . .
Just ahead of Christmas the Sun moves on and heralds a month long period when you are definitely out there in the forefront of life. Few could doubt your energy or determination and there are plenty of new possibilities about, both socially and in terms of romance. Keep pushing forward now.

23 WEDNESDAY   *Moon Age Day 4 • Moon Sign Aquarius*

am . . . .

pm . . . .
There are all sorts of ideas coming from a number of different people today. The trouble is that all of them appear to make a great deal of sense and so it is difficult to know which ones to opt for. When you have looked at everything carefully you are inclined to choose your own path in any case.

24 THURSDAY   *Moon Age Day 5 • Moon Sign Pisces*

am . . . .

pm . . . .
It's Christmas Eve already and you might be feeling that you are far from ready for what the days ahead are going to demand from you. You need to get one thing straight: Anything that hasn't been done by now you can easily manage without. Placing yourself under stress is not to be recommended.

25 FRIDAY   *Moon Age Day 6 • Moon Sign Pisces*

am..

pm..
A particularly good Christmas Day for most of you, with a variety of
possibilities and much love coming from the direction of the people you
care about the most. Later in the day you may come face to face with
someone from the dim and distant past. Memories are an important part
of the day.

26 SATURDAY   *Moon Age Day 7 • Moon Sign Pisces*

am..

pm..
With a little more time to think about things today, you are bringing
certain facts into focus in a way that was not possible when you were so
busy practically speaking. This allows a sideways look at life and may
lead to some fairly radical behaviour once the Christmas period is over.

27 SUNDAY   *Moon Age Day 8 • Moon Sign Aries*

am..

pm..
A little peace and quiet is likely to be what you are looking for today,
though whether you actually find it remains to be seen. The trouble is
that your popularity is so high that everyone wants to include you in
their own version of the celebrations. Don't spread yourself too thinly
however.

| ← NEGATIVE TREND | | | | | | POSITIVE TREND → | | | | |
-5	-4	-3	-2	-1		+1	+2	+3	+4	+5
					LOVE					
					MONEY					
					LUCK					
					VITALITY					

28 MONDAY

Moon Age Day 9 • Moon Sign Aries

am . . . .

pm . . . .
It won't be long before the Moon finds itself in your sign again, so if you lack lustre at the start of today, energy levels will certainly rise later on. Take some time out in the morning to please yourself and if you are back at work already, try not to push yourself too hard for a day or two.

29 TUESDAY

Moon Age Day 10 • Moon Sign Taurus

am . . . .

pm . . . .
With the lunar high offering everything to play for, and new possibilities inhabiting every sphere of your life, you are already looking ahead to the New Year and what it might offer you personally. A good day to make decisions and to push ahead just as positively as you can.

30 WEDNESDAY

Moon Age Day 11 • Moon Sign Taurus

am . . . .

pm . . . .
It might seem as if some of the incentives surrounding you at this time are wasted, mainly because it's impossible to get other people motivated ahead of the New Year celebrations. All you can do is to shelve certain plans and to gather your resources to create a great time socially.

31 THURSDAY

Moon Age Day 12 • Moon Sign Gemini

am . . . .

pm . . . .
Although the last day of the year does not represent an anticlimax, it might not be quite as exciting as you had wished. The truth is that you have already passed the change and are well into the potential for the year ahead already. You start 1999 in a position of strength and determination.

RISING SIGNS
for TAURUS

Look along the top to find your date of birth, and down the side for hour (or two) if appropriate for Summer Time.

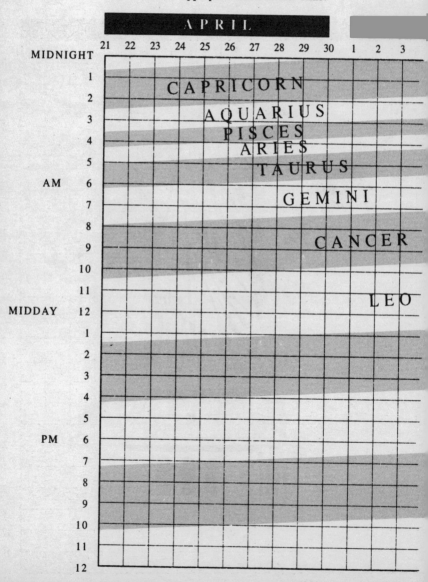

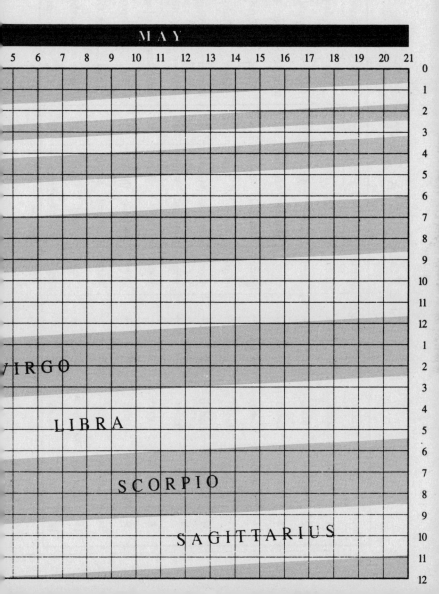

	MAY															
5	6	7	8	9	10	11	12	13	14	15	16	17	18	19	20	21

VIRGO

LIBRA

SCORPIO

SAGITTARIUS

THE ZODIAC AT A GLANCE

Placed	Sign	Symbol	Glyph	Polarity	Element	Quality	Planet	Glyph	Metal	Stone	Opposite
1	Aries	Ram	♈	+	Fire	Cardinal	Mars	♂	Iron	Bloodstone	Libra
2	Taurus	Bull	♉	−	Earth	Fixed	Venus	♀	Copper	Sapphire	Scorpio
3	Gemini	Twins	♊	+	Air	Mutable	Mercury	☿	Mercury	Tiger's Eye	Sagittarius
4	Cancer	Crab	♋	−	Water	Cardinal	Moon	☽	Silver	Pearl	Capricorn
5	Leo	Lion	♌	+	Fire	Fixed	Sun	☉	Gold	Ruby	Aquarius
6	Virgo	Maiden	♍	−	Earth	Mutable	Mercury	☿	Mercury	Sardonyx	Pisces
7	Libra	Scales	♎	+	Air	Cardinal	Venus	♀	Copper	Sapphire	Aries
8	Scorpio	Scorpion	♏	−	Water	Fixed	Pluto	♇	Plutonium	Jasper	Taurus
9	Sagittarius	Archer	♐	+	Fire	Mutable	Jupiter	♃	Tin	Topaz	Gemini
10	Capricorn	Goat	♑	−	Earth	Cardinal	Saturn	♄	Lead	Black Onyx	Cancer
11	Aquarius	Waterbearer	♒	+	Air	Fixed	Uranus	♅	Uranium	Amethyst	Leo
12	Pisces	Fishes	♓	−	Water	Mutable	Neptune	♆	Tin	Moonstone	Virgo

THE ZODIAC, PLANETS AND CORRESPONDENCES

In the first column of the table of correspondence, I list the signs of the Zodiac as they order themselves around their circle; starting with Aries and finishing with Pisces. In the last column, I list the signs as they will appear as opposites to those in the first column. For example, the sign which will be positioned opposite Aries, in a circular chart will be Libra.

Each sign of the Zodiac is either positive or negative. This by no means suggests that they are either 'good' or 'bad', but that they are either extrovert, outgoing, masculine signs (positive), or introspective, receptive, feminine signs (negative).

Each sign of the Zodiac will belong to one of the four Elements: Fire, Air, Earth or Water. Fire signs are creative and enthusiastic; Air signs are mentally active and thoughtful; Earth signs are constructive and practical; Water signs are emotional and have strong feelings.

Each sign of the Zodiac also belongs to one of the Qualities: Cardinal, Fixed or Mutable. Cardinal signs are initiators and pioneers; Fixed signs are consistent and inflexible; Mutable signs are educators and live to serve.

So, each sign will be either positive or negative, and will belong to one of the Elements and to one of the Qualities. You can see from the table, for example, that Aries is a positive, Cardinal, Fire sign.

The table also shows which planets rule each sign. For example, Mars is the ruling planet of Aries. Each planet represents a particular facet of personality - Mars represents physical energy and drive - and the sign which it rules is the one with which it has most in common,

The table also shows which metals and gem stones are associated with, or correspond with the signs of the Zodiac. Again, the correspondence is made when a metal or stone possesses properties that are held in common with a particular sign of the Zodiac. This system of correspondences can be extended to encompass any group, whether animal, vegetable or mineral - as well as people! For example, each sign of the Zodiac is associated with particular flowers and herbs, with particular animals, with particular towns and countries, and so on.

It is an interesting exercise when learning about astrology, to guess which sign of the Zodiac rules a particular thing, by trying to match its qualities with the appropriate sign.

0891 229 723: *ring Old Moore now* – for the most authentic personal phone horoscope ever made available

Then just tap in your own birth date . . .

. . . and benefit from the wisdom of the centuries

The uncanny foresights of Britain's Nº1 astrologer – focused directly on your own <u>individual</u> birth-chart

Unique personalised reading

There's never been a better way to exploit your personal horoscope opportunities.

Old Moore now has a massive new computer with which he can produce a personal forecast based on the actual day of your birth. No other phone service can produce this level of accuracy. But then again, you would expect Old Moore to be ahead of the pack.

Any day of the week, Old Moore can update you on the planetary influences which surround you and point up the opportunities which will be open to you.

Unique record of prediction

The principles of astral interpretation laid down by Old Moore three centuries ago have proved amazingly reliable and accurate right up to the present day. That's how the Almanac continues to astound the world, year after year. And that's how the Old Moore system can be harnessed to the analysis of your own personal world.

Your weekly rendezvous with Old Moore

For just 36p per minute* you can hear this authoritative overview of your life, work and happiness, complete with advice on lucky dates and numbers, and the charting of your energy rhythms. Not the usual 'fortune-telling' patter. But enlightened insights into how best to exploit the future.

Remember, unlike any other phone-astrologer, Old Moore will ask you for the *day, month and year* of your birth. To give you the most individual predictions ever made possible at the lift of a phone.

So touch hands with the immortal Old Moore. Ring this number and get the benefit of a truly personalised forecast, based on the world's most acclaimed astrological tradition.

This service is only available on a touch tone button phone.

0891 229 723

*Calls cost 39p per minute cheap rate, 49p at all other times.